Children's rights in a transitional society

Children's rights in a transitional society

Proceedings of a conference hosted by the Centre for Child Law in Pretoria, 30 October 1998

Edited by CJ Davel

Protea Book House
1999

Children's Rights in a Transitional Society

Protea Book House
PO Box 35110,
Menlopark 0102
protea@intekom.co.za

© Centre for Child Law
University of Pretoria
and Potchefstroomse
Universiteit vir CHO

Design: HOND BK
Reproduction:
Dusk Dimensions
Printed: Interpak

First edition
First print
1999

ISBN 0-620-24626-X

© All rights reserved. No reproduction in any form is allowed without the written permission of the publisher and the Centre for Child Law, University of Pretoria and Potchefstroomse Universiteit vir CHO.

THE South African society is a society in transition. The transition had an impact on children's rights. The question to be answered in this publication is whether that impact is sufficient.

- **Minister Tshabalala-Msimang** pledges the sincerity of government and gives a brief outline on what has been done in this regard.
- **Carolyn Hamilton** deals with the internationally accepted standards pertaining to children. South Africa has ratified the United Nation Convention on the Rights of the Child and it is therefore compelling that we adhere to these requirements.
- **Lilian Edwards** deals with the basic question whether the voice of children can effectively be heard in the law. This contribution draws on the recent experience of the Scottish legal system and its attempts to implement the participation rights of the child as guaranteed by article 12 of the Convention.
- **June Sinclair** indicates the paradigm shift that took place, i.e. from parental rights to children's rights.
- In theory the children of South Africa have rights protecting them, but **Tshidi Mayimele-Hashatse** indicates that child labour is still a problem in the country affecting millions of children.
- **Ann Skelton** describes the unfinished journey of juvenile justice reform in South Africa and identifies and examines three major themes which have influenced the process of law reform, namely children's rights, restorative justice and political will.
- **Julia Sloth-Nielsen** and **Belinda van Heerden** deals with the process of establishing a comprehensive Children's Statute for South Africa – breaking away from the piece meal legislation of the past and dealing with significant features e.g. the democratisation of the family, etc.
- The editor, **Trynie Davel**, is the director of the Centre for Child Law and a professor of Private Law at the University of Pretoria.

CONTENTS

Foreword
Manto Tshabalala-Msimang (Minister of Health)
— page 7

Implementing children's rights in a transitional society
Carolyn Hamilton (University of Essex, UK)
— page 13

Hearing the voice of the child: notes from the Scottish experience
Lilian Edwards (Edinburgh University, Scotland)
— page 37

From parents' rights to children's rights
June Sinclair (University of Pretoria)
— page 62

Child labour
Tshidi Mayimele-Hashatse (Attorney, Sandton)
— page 80

Juvenile justice reform: children's rights and responsibilities versus crime control
Ann Skelton (Lawyers for Human Rights, Pietermaritzburg)
— page 88

The political economy of child law reform: pie in the sky?
Julia Sloth-Nielson (University of the Western Cape) and
Belinda van Heerden (University of Cape Town)
— page 107

United Nations International Convention on the Rights of the Child
—page 129

Foreword

Dr Manto Tshabalala-Msimang*

Let me first congratulate the Faculty of Law at the University of Pretoria and the Faculty of Law at the Potchefstroomse Universiteit vir Christelike Hoër Onderwys in the launching of the Centre for Child Law. It is indeed an honour and privilege for me to be afforded the opportunity to deliver the opening address. We in government and the Department of Justice look forward to a close working relationship with your centre. The sharing of information and expertise, and the linking up with other international institutions is imperative in our striving towards a better future for all our children. Your centre's commitment to collaborate closely with various other tertiary institutions and NGOs is therefore commended.

Children and the youth of our country were not spared the pain and trauma of the violation of their rights, and in a way they continue to experience the legacy of the past in the violation of their rights. Glaring in this regard is the trafficking in children and child abuse.

This conference is aptly called 'Children's rights in a transitional society'. In fact, Schedule 6 of our Constitution that deals with transitional arrangements clearly emphasises the transitional element in our society and section 28 makes provision for the promotion and protection of children's rights.

What attention is given to children's rights in this process of transformation? What priorities must be given to the development and implementation of children's rights in relation to other rights, taking into account the injustices of the past. The

---

* Minister of Health, formerly, Deputy Minister of Justice.

answer is a simple one: the same as all the other rights enshrined in our Constitution. The government is duty bound to respect, protect, promote and fulfil the rights embodied in the Bill of Rights. The inclusion in die Bill of Rights of a section on children ensures that the government must give equal attention to all the rights contained therein.

Whilst the answer is a simple one, giving proper effect thereto is just the opposite. However, the government has accepted this challenge, and dare I say, we are on our way.

As we are all aware, when the government of South Africa ratified the United Nations Convention on the Rights of the Child (hereafter 'the UN Convention on the Rights of the Child') on 16 June 1995, it committed itself and the people of South Africa to a new respect for all children, thereby placing a new emphasis on the justice system in all matters affecting them. To this end the government has indeed begun a process of implementing the principle of a 'First call for children' whereby the needs of children are considered paramount throughout the government's programmes, services and development strategies.

Our children are tomorrow's leaders, workers, scientists and parents. This means that their survival, health, nutrition, education and protection must be seen as a key priority area in the building of a new democratic South Africa.

These basic needs of our children are linked to the question of rights and that is our moral obligation to the children of South Africa. This finds expression firstly in the new South African Constitution and in particular in section 28 of the Constitution, which is indeed a milestone in our history and secondly in the ratification of the UN Convention on the Rights of the Child. Children are now entitled to all the constitutional guarantees, the cornerstone of which is respect for human dignity and equality before the law.

The principles embodied in the Constitution, the UN Convention on the Rights of the Child and other human rights instruments should underlie all legislative reforms. The sectoral and inter-sectoral programmes that are being put in place form an integral part of a process of beginning to realise the protection of the rights of the child. The National Programme of Action for Children (NPA) is an excellent example of this intersectoral participation. This is a mechanism for identifying all plans geared towards child protection and development by the government, non-governmental organisations and other child-related structures, and for ensuring that all these plans are developed within the framework of the Constitution, the UN Convention on the Rights of the Child, the goals of the 1990 World Summit for Children and other human rights instruments.

We, both the government and civil society, have realised commendable strides in guaranteeing the protection of our children. However, much more needs to be done with the children and for the children, especially against the backdrop of our report on the implementation of the UN Convention on the Rights of the Child. In the department of Justice, for instance, through the process of developing a National Programme of Action for Children, the South African Law Commission has established a number of project committees that are carrying out important investigations on the protection of children. There are project committees on the establishment of a child justice system and sexual offences against children, and a review of the Child Care Act. Often the criminal justice system has been very harsh to children. In fact, for some children it has been a harrowing experience.

Thus investigations into the establishment of the child justice system will certainly aim to promote the well-being of the child, and to deal with each child in an individualised way. It is envisaged that the central focus of this new system will be on the diversion of children away from the criminal justice system as early as possible, either to the welfare system, or to suitable diversion programmes run by competent staff. The involvement of the family and community is of vital importance, as is sensitivity to culture, tradition and the empowerment of victims. I am very eager to see this project materialise as a matter of priority.

In the department of Justice a directorate has been established on gender and children's issues. This directorate is responsible, amongst other things, for facilitating the implementation of the National Programme of Action for Children and the UN Convention on the Rights of the Child. Through this mechanism, I see the promotion of educational material for children on their rights in relation to the justice system as a core function of the children's programme in the department of Justice.

In order to attain the goals which we have set for ourselves in the National Programme of Action and other related structures, we need to promote and strengthen the partnerships within government departments and between government departments and organisations in society that are involved in the administration of justice.

Addressing the many vital issues relating to children requires not only the simple removal of obsolete and discriminatory legislation, but also positive and pro-active action. Hence changing laws and policies is not enough. Further action is required in order to ensure that progressive laws and policies are translated into real change on the ground. We must therefore put our heads together to ensure that these wonderful pieces of legislation and policies that aim to protect the child are not just pieces of paper but do indeed become a reality.

Let us briefly refer to the HIV/Aids epidemic, a crisis facing our country, and how it impacts on the children and youth of our country. Globally it is estimated that by 1998, 600 000 children will have been infected with HIV. Eight and a half million children will have been orphaned. Of every ten children orphaned as a result of Aids, nine are in sub-Saharan Africa. We are not sure how many children in South Africa have been orphaned, but it is estimated that to date there are about 200 000 orphaned children in South Africa as a result of Aids. What is the future of these children? Can we afford another marginalised generation? The government's initiative of partnerships against Aids seeks to foster a culture of working together to make a difference and protect ourselves and particularly our children from the spread of HIV/Aids.

Our national action plan to improve the promotion and protection of human rights is our response, as the government, to the recommendation of the Vienna Declaration and Programme of Action adopted at the World Conference on Human Rights in Vienna in 1993. These required that each state consider the desirability of drawing up a national action plan identifying steps whereby the state would improve the protection and promotion of human rights.

Our national action plan to be lodged with the United Nations in New York on 10 December 1998, international Human Rights Day, identifies comprehensive plans to promote and protect children's rights. These will also be given prominence at the celebrations of Human Rights Day nationally, through activities that will focus on children's rights.

The exploitation of children in South Africa generally relates to the extreme inequality of economic circumstances. The primary thrust in reducing exploitation should therefore include programmes on education and job creation. The national job summit is therefore also of extreme importance. One of the aims of this summit would be to create a sufficient number of jobs to match the net growth in the labour force and to expand special employment programmes to raise the level of job creation as quickly as possible. This national job summit can therefore be seen as a significant step towards alleviating poverty and thereby improving the situation of our children.

I would like to conclude with unequivocal support of the following ideal that appeared in the *Progress of Nations Report* of 1997, published by the United Nations Children's Fund:

'The day will come when nations will be judged not by their military or economic strength, nor by the splendour of their capital cities and public buildings, but by the well-being of their peoples; by their levels of health, nutrition and education; by their opportunities to earn a fair reward for their labours; by their ability to participate in the decisions that affect their lives; by the respect that is shown for their civil and political liberties; by the provision that is made for those who are vulnerable and disadvantaged; and by the protection that is afforded to the growing minds and bodies of their children.'

Implementing children's rights in a transitional society

Prof Carolyn Hamilton*

1　INTRODUCTION

South Africa has experienced enormous political and social change during the 1990s: apartheid has been deposed, democracy has been embraced, and there has emerged a growing recognition of the importance of human rights. However, the impact such changes will have on children and the extent to which this new political and philosophical climate will bring about the implementation of the rights contained in the UN Convention on the Rights of the Child is not as yet clear.

There are approximately 19 million children in the Republic of South Africa, comprising around 45% of the population.[1] Children have not been shielded from the political upheavals and the social disruption caused by the previous apartheid system of government. Indeed, the South African report submitted to the UN Committee on the Rights of the Child in 1997 points out that children have been the victims of gross human rights violations, including separation from parents, abduction, rape, imprisonment without trial and persecution for their beliefs.[2] Large numbers of children grew up under the apartheid

---

*　Director of the Children's Legal Centre, University of Essex, UK.
1　The 1991 census only gives figures for those aged 0-19, thus including 18 year olds. The figure expressed in the text above is an estimation of the population excluding 18 year olds. The initial country report submitted to the UN Committee on the Rights of the Child does not include the figures from the 1996 census. It is believed that the child population has risen as a proportion of the population in the last decade.
2　*Focus on Children and Youth* Truth and Reconciliation Commission, May 1997 and Submission to the Truth and Reconciliation Commission by National Children and Violence Trust, June 1997.

regime in an environment where violence, fear and oppression were part of everyday life. As the report acknowledges, the challenge for the future will be to find ways to heal, rehabilitate and restore; to build a culture of respect and to redress the imbalances created by the trauma experienced by so many children. It is a challenge that cannot be ignored by South Africa.[3] The state, especially a state in a transitional society, relies very heavily on its next generation, its children, to embrace the ideas of democracy and human rights and carry them forward as the lynch-pin of the political and social system.

South Africa is obviously not alone in this respect. The aim of this article is to examine the development of the UN Convention on the Rights of the Child and the extent to which the convention may be used as a tool to bring about an improvement in children's rights.

1.1 Background to the UN Convention on the Rights of the Child

It may come as a surprise to many to learn that the UN Convention on the Rights of the Child is the most widely ratified human rights instrument in the world. As it approaches the tenth anniversary of its creation, only two states have yet to ratify this convention.[4]

The process of drafting the UN Convention on the Rights of the Child was slow and tortuous. The initial idea of a convention for children's rights was raised by the Polish delegation in a proposal submitted to the 34th session of the United Nations Commission of Human Rights in 1978.[5] The Convention was seen as an appropriate way of marking the International Year of the Child in 1979 and a means of strengthening the 1959 Declaration on the Rights of the Child. The justification for the proposal was, as the Polish delegation put it, the

---

3 See *Initial Country Report South Africa Convention on the Rights of the Child* November 1997, Introduction.
4 These are Somalia and the USA. The latter state is a signatory but has not, as yet, ratified the Convention.
5 UN CHR 1978a:1-5.

need to 'further strengthen the comprehensive care and well-being of children all over the world.'[6] The proposal, however, was not accompanied by any convincing evidence of the need for a convention rather than a declaration. The Polish delegation did not submit evidence that there were specific deficiencies in the existing provision for children's rights or a lack of appropriate mechanisms for ensuring their rights.[7] This appears, at first glance, rather a surprising omission. However, the approach of the Polish government reflected and illustrated the general attitude to children's rights at the time. So little attention had been given to the needs of children as a separate group or separate population, that it would have been difficult to produce direct evidence of the failure of human rights instruments to protect them adequately.

There was, for instance, little in the way of child-focused statistical evidence available on the position of children in the 1970s.[8] Statistics on children were rarely disaggregated from those relating to adults. Further, what was proposed by the Polish delegation was a convention with virtually the same articles as the 1959 Declaration: in other words, the proposal was a status-raising exercise: to raise to convention status an already existing declaration.

The Polish delegation's proposal for a convention on the rights of children was not greeted with any noticeable enthusiasm. Some questioned whether a convention was really necessary, especially in view of the fact that the proposed convention largely reiterated the UN Declaration on the Rights of the Child 1959. Others asked whether it was the right time for the drafting and adopting of such a convention, especially in view of the projects and research that were planned for the International Year of the Child.

---

6 UN CHR 1978a:1, 1978b:10.
7 See N Cantwell 'The Origins, Development and Significance of the UN Convention on the Rights of the Child' in *United Nations Convention on the Rights of the Child: A Guide to the Travaux Preparatoires* (ed) S Detrick (ed), Dordrecht, Martinus Nijhoff, 1992 at 19.
8 Poland had a long-term interest in children's rights. It was a Polish diplomat who had ensured the continuation of UNICEF once its post Second World War mandate to care for war-displaced children had expired.

The idea of protective instruments aimed specifically at children was not new. From the beginning of the 20th century, and more particularly from the end of the First World War, the need to provide protection for children was clearly on the agenda of regional and international drafting bodies. It could be seen in such instruments as the:
- International Convention for the Suppression of the White Slave Traffic 1910;
- ILO Conventions Fixing the Minimum Age for Admission of Children to Industrial Employment 1919;
- ILO Convention Concerning the Night Work of Young Persons Employed in Industry 1919;
- International Convention for the Suppression of Traffic in Women and Children 1921;
- Children's Charter of the International Convention of Women 1922;
- Declaration of Geneva 1924;
- Children's Charter of President Hoover's White House Conference on Child Health and Protection 1930;
- Bill of Rights for the Handicapped Child;
- Children's Charter in Wartime;
- Children's Charter for the Post-war World 1942;
- Declaration of the Opportunities for Children 1942 and
- Declaration on the Rights of the Child 1959.

The problem with these instruments was that they had made little noticeable impact on the position of children globally. Many were aspirational rather than instruments that could be practically implemented. The 1959 Declaration consisted of a preamble and ten principles. This declaration was notable, however, in that it declared a child to be the holder of rights, rather than a person who was simply entitled to certain services and protections. The declaration stated that a child is entitled to a name and nationality, adequate nutrition, housing, recreation and medical services, and to be 'among the first' to receive protection and relief. Its principles were, however, limited.

It did not contain any civil or political rights for children, contrary to the wishes of those states who wanted, at the time of the drafting, to expand the range of coverage in the instrument. For instance, the Soviet Union put forward a proposal to include the prohibition on corporal punishment in schools, but this and other proposals to extend coverage failed to gain acceptance.[9]

The initial Polish proposal for a child rights convention was, essentially, a reiteration of the existing Declaration on the Rights of the Child with an additional implementation mechanism. It had nine substantive articles. However, many of the state delegates pointed out that the two major covenants, the International Covenant on Civil and Political Rights[10] and the Covenant on Social Economic and Cultural Rights already provided children with most of these rights. Indeed, article 24 of the International Covenant on Civil and Political Rights specifically addressed children and provided that every child had the right to protection without discrimination, the right to be registered immediately after birth and the right to have a name and to acquire a nationality.

Those lobbying for a proposed convention on children's rights argued that such articles were not enough. Like those who had earlier lobbied for the Convention on the Elimination of all Forms of Discrimination against Women, they argued that while the covenants technically covered children, in the sense that they covered all persons, and while the rights contained in the covenant were, by and large, equally applicable to them, these instruments did not adequately address the needs of this vulnerable and largely powerless group of humans.

Interestingly, the NGOs were not entirely supportive of the Polish delegation's proposals. However, their reasons were rather different from those of the states that objected. They felt

---

9 See UN Doc E/Cn5/111. At the time of drafting the declaration, the Polish delegation had tried unsuccessfully to propose a legally binding treaty rather than a non-binding declaration.
10 Children's rights were included in this convention in article 24. The inclusion of this article was also a Polish initiative.

that a possible convention needed more consideration. They wanted to wait until the conclusion of the International Year of the Child with its anticipated supporting studies and projects before considering a convention for children .

In the face of the concerns raised by state delegates and NGOs and, in a spirit of compromise, the Commission on Human Rights called for the conclusion of a convention on the rights of the child 'if possible' at the 35th Session of the Commission on Human Rights in 1979. In the intervening period, the Secretary-General invited member states of the UN, IGOs and NGOs[11] to submit observations and recommendations in response to the draft.

This delay led to a very different children's rights convention than had been originally envisaged by the Polish delegation. States were afforded the opportunity to examine the Polish proposal much more carefully and many found it wanting. The Polish delegation were themselves aware of this problem and produced a second draft of a possible convention in 1979. This amended draft contained twenty substantive articles. The end product, and the convention that finally received approval, was different again from this proposal, with twice as many substantive articles.

But the second proposed draft convention marked a real shift from an essentially protection-based instrument, where children were receivers of services or protection, to children being regarded as the holders of a full range of rights.

During the eleven years from the initial proposal and the ten years from the establishment of a working group by the UN Commission on Human Rights to oversee the drafting of the convention, there was a sea change in thinking about the concept of children's rights. For instance, the western states recognised the need for the state to protect children in and from their families,[12] and also accepted that children needed to be inter-

---

11 The NGOs consulted were those who had consultative status to ECOSOC.
12 The battered child syndrome was only really accepted at the end of the 1960s with the development of sophisticated x-ray techniques. Sexual abuse of children in the family was only accepted and recognised widely during the 1970s.

active participants in education if standards were to improve. This was also a time when western democracy as a political ideal was gaining ground at the expense of communism as a dominant political ideology.

For those working in the field of children's rights, the convention represents a real shift in philosophy, content and practice. Previous documents had concentrated on the protection of children. Unlike the 1959 Declaration or the 1924 Geneva Declaration, the UN Convention on the Rights of the Child covers not just 'protection rights' but economic, social and cultural rights as well as civil and political rights. It places considerable burdens and restrictions on a state's ability to set policy in dealing with children.

1.2 The UN Convention on the Rights of the Child

The Convention is underpinned by three principles: the right of children not to be discriminated against,[13] the right to participate in decisions affecting their lives and to be heard,[14] and the 'best interests' concept which means that in all actions concerning children, whether undertaken by public or private social welfare institutions, courts of law, administrative authorities or legislative bodies, the best interests of the child shall be a primary consideration.[15] The Convention provisions are generally categorised into three parts: rights of protection; rights of provision and rights of participation, as illustrated below. The most interesting new 'right' or guiding principle is the right of children to be heard and to participate in decisions affecting their lives. The drafters of this Convention hoped that the Convention would receive universal ratification by the year 2000. It is unlikely that this deadline will be achieved. Neither Somalia nor the USA have ratified it, nor are they likely to by the end of the year. The USA cannot meet the Convention obligations, especially those relating to juvenile justice and Somalia does not have a government structure at present which would permit ratification.

---

13 Article 2.
14 Article 12.
15 Article 3.

The Convention on the Rights of the Child: Guiding principles and rights

NON-DISCRIMINATION
|
BEST INTERESTS OF THE CHILD
|
RIGHT TO BE HEARD, TO HAVE VIEWS TAKEN INTO ACCOUNT
|

PROTECTION	PROVISION	PARTICIPATION
• From abuse and neglect	• Right to survival and development	• Freedom of expression
• From exploitation (in the economic/sexual/social sense)	• Right to highest level of health possible, access to health and medical services	• Freedom of thought, conscience, religion
• Special protection for children deprived of families	• Access to appropriate information	• Freedom of association
• Protection from labour market exploitation, torture, unlawful arrest, deprivation of liberty, preservation of identity	• Right to benefit from social security	• Right to make views known
	• Right to an adequate standard of living	• Right to be heard in judicial or administrative proceedings
• Right to a name and nationality	• Right to education	
• Special protection for child refugees	• Right of minorities to enjoy their own culture	
• Protection from drug abuse	• Right to leisure, play and participation in cultural and leisure activities	
	• Right to rehabilitative care	

Nonetheless, children's organisations, both international and national, that lobbied hard for the Convention can regard the rate of ratification with some self-congratulation.

However, complacency would be misplaced. Some hard questions have to be asked: in particular, has ratification brought about a significant change in the status and well-being of children; to what extent do states actually implement the Convention; and how effective are the monitoring and implementation mechanisms?

When the two year post-ratification reports of states to the Committee on the Rights of the Child are examined and the concluding observations made by the committee taken into account, it is clear that none of the states whose reports have been considered so far has implemented the Convention to the total satisfaction of the committee.

All the reporting states have been subject to a degree of criticism for their failure to implement the provisions of the Convention fully. Perhaps, given the range of rights contained in the Convention and the changes in law, practice and policy required, this was to be expected, especially in transitional states. The real indication of the willingness of states to progress to full implementation will be seen in the second wave of reports required to be submitted to the committee, five years after ratification.

While the Convention reflects a real change in the way children's rights are viewed by the international community and is clearly an instrument which takes children's rights to a new level, the Convention has not been an unqualified success. A number of criticisms have been levelled at the Convention. In particular, the provisions relating to monitoring mechanisms and the implementation of the Convention are weak.

There are, for instance, no agreed monitoring indicators to measure a state's successful implementation of the rights contained in the Convention. Further, the articles detailing the nature of the rights are, on occasion, so general that they may do little to improve the status of children or sufficiently enhance their life opportunities.

2 MONITORING AND IMPLEMENTATION

The monitoring mechanisms of the Convention are found in articles 42 to 45. Monitoring occurs primarily through review of a state report, submitted to the UN Committee on the Rights of the Child. NGOs may submit supplementary reports to that of the state, which will also be considered by the committee. In reviewing the report the task of the committee is 'to examine the progress made by State parties in achieving the realisation of the obligations undertaken in the present Convention'.[16] The purpose of the examination of state reports by the committee is to open a dialogue with states to check which rights have been implemented and which have not. Implementation of obligations is viewed as a progressive and collaborative process rather than an adversarial process.[17] Further, the view taken is that monitoring should focus on the measurement of achievements ongoing and improving over time, rather than highlighting shortcomings.[18]

Although the Committee on the Rights of the Child has laid down guidelines for states to follow when compiling their reports,[19] these guidelines are very general. Abramson has pointed out that

> 'One glaring inadequacy of the guidelines is that they do not ask States for any information on spending. Even the most elementary questions about what percentages of a State's budget go to children's health or education are omitted. States merely are "encouraged" to provide relevant statistical information and indicators'.[20]

---

16 See S Detrick *Travaux Preparatoires to the Convention on the Rights of the Child* Kluwer 1992 at 555.
17 P Alston 'Out of the Abyss: the Challenges Confronting the New UN Committee on Economic, Social and Cultural Rights' (1987) 9 *Human Rights Quarterly* 332.
18 This is the view taken by Himes 'Reflections on Indicators Concerning the Rights of the Child: the Development and Human Rights Communities should get their Acts Together' paper for seminar on 'Appropriate Indicators to Measure Achievements in the Progressive Realisation of Economic, Social and Cultural Rights' Geneva 25-29 January 1993.
19 UN Doc 15 July 1991.
20 'First State Reports: Sunny and ... cloudy' *International Children's Rights Monitor* vol 10 nos 1-2 at 23. South Africa, however, is one of the few states to issue a children's budget.

Further, there is a lack of any accepted minimum standards or yardsticks against which progress can be measured. Both the state wishing to implement the Convention and international bodies charged with monitoring the convention would have benefited from the establishment of such benchmarks.[21] Judith Ennew states:

> 'The Committee on the Rights of the Child ... [is] a foster mother to the Convention on the Rights of the Child, charged with its nurture through implementation on the one hand, while on the other encouraging the parenting skills of the ratifying states. The main issues are thus those of clarifying norms, developing concepts specifying the core content of rights and of indicators to measure their progressive realisation, as well as encouraging political will at national and international levels.'[22]

Even the core contents of rights have not been identified by the committee. Thus, for instance, there has been no decision on the age at which states should treat children as being criminally responsible: only statements that so low an age as ten is viewed as being a matter of concern.[23] Likewise, there has been no indication from the committee as to the proportion of a state's budget that should be applied to children or any agreement as to how many years education constitutes an acceptable primary education.

Having reviewed a report, the committee, together with the reporting government and any aid agencies involved, should attempt to define the problems and discuss what remedies are necessary. However, few states, whether first world, transitional or third world, will admit readily to problems that cannot be handled by their own national mechanisms. Indeed,

---

[21] The first Working Group established by ECOSOC to monitor the implementation of the International Covenant on Economic, Social and Cultural Rights failed to establish standards for the rights concerned in that covenant.
[22] *Monitoring the Convention on the Rights of the Child* Report for Radda Barnen, March 1993.
[23] See Concluding Observations on UK Report UN Doc.

some states are not even willing to acknowledge that there has been anything other than full implementation of children's rights in their state.[24] It is obviously difficult for a state to be self-critical, even in the face of what may be construed as fairly strident comment from the committee.[25]

A further problem is that of late reports. The committee cannot engage in effective dialogue with a state without its submission of a report. There are some states which have not even submitted a first report, due two years after ratification.

This is particularly unfortunate as this number includes states in which there are considerable existing concerns about the implementation of children's rights, for example, Afghanistan (due 26 April 1996), Angola (due 3 January 1993), Bahrain (due 12 March 1994), Bosnia and Herzegovina (due 5 March 1994), Brazil (due 23 October 1992), Estonia (due 19 November 1993), Eritrea (1 September 1996), Israel (due 1 November 1993), Kenya (due 1 September 1992) and Tanzania (due 9 July 1993). One might argue that the failure to submit reports makes a mockery of the process of implementation through dialogue and constructive encouragement. It also makes the claim to virtual universal ratification somewhat hollow in terms of the realisation of children's rights.

Given the difficulties faced by the committee – an inability to insist on reports, the lack of resources to give sufficient time to consideration of reports and the need for dialogue to promote rights – there may be little that the committee can do to bring about effective change for some of the most vulnerable children. Indeed, Ennew concludes that the whole idea of state reporting as a means of implementation and monitoring may be time-consuming, expensive, ineffectual and of dubious value.[26]

---

24 See for instance, the Report of Sudan which states that 'The Sudanes family never uses ill-treatment or violence, in accordance with the teachings and precepts of religion' at 21.
25 In the case of the UK, the first state report was the subject of considerable criticism by the Committee on the Rights of the Child. The then Conservative government refused to admit that there were issues of implementation of children's rights that were anything less than satisfactory.
26 Ibid at 7.

In contrast to the European Convention of Human Rights, which has been an effective instrument for implementing children's rights, the Convention on the Rights of the Child does not include a complaints mechanism nor a right of individual petition. The effect of this omission is that enforcement mechanisms remain weak. Virtually the only mechanism for reproving a state which fails to implement the convention is that of negative publicity or public 'shaming'. To a large extent this lack of enforcement mechanism was a conscious choice. The drafters and the Committee on the Rights of the Child saw and continue to see change and implementation of the Convention coming about through negotiation and consensus, with perhaps some general persuasion, not least from the bad publicity that flows from any critical concluding observations by the committee on a state report.

Because the committee may only comment on a particular state's actions and implementation of the Convention when a report is submitted by that state, the committee cannot comment on gross violations being perpetrated against children if a state report is not before them. An attempt was made to remedy this very restricted role of the Committee on the Rights of the Child during its second session in 1992. The members of the committee agreed that apart from the examination of state reports, it should have the authority to undertake urgent actions in serious situations.[27] However, the committee accepted that before any 'urgent action' could be taken, certain conditions would have to be met: the action would have to be based on reliable information; a violation of the rights contained in the Convention on the Rights of the Child would have to be involved and be taking place within the jurisdiction of a state party; the violation concerned would have to be blatant and there would have to be a real danger that further violations would take place in the future. Urgent action would only be taken where it would be possible to avoid a deterioration of the situation.[28]

---

27 CRC/C/10 paras 54-58.
28 CRC/C/20 no 156.

Such stringent conditions, especially the requirement that a 'blatant violation' must have already occurred, with a real danger of further serious violations, would mean that the committee could only intervene at a very late stage, when violations had already taken place and when it would be extremely difficult to reverse or improve the situation. Further, the 'urgent action' to be taken by the committee would consist of passing on information and bringing the violations to the notice of other appropriate organs of the UN.

Overall the 'urgent action' procedure was envisaged as being non-conflictual and a mode of opening dialogue before a state was required to submit a report. Such 'urgent action' is unlikely to have a great impact on children's life opportunities, particularly once conflict has started or a government has adopted policies which violate children's rights.[29] The committee's inability to be in the forefront of bringing violations of children's rights to a state's notice reduces considerably its ability to bring about 'implementation' and to exert moral pressure on state parties.

The committee's inability to be a pro-active protector of children's rights or a pro-active rather than reactive publicist of violations of children's rights is largely due to the nature of the Convention, the monitoring mechanisms and the role that the committee sees itself as playing.

Thomas Hammarberg, one of the original members of the Committee on the Rights of the Child, saw the Convention not as a judicial instrument which would allow intervention to remedy violations of children's rights, but rather as a political instrument to bring about changes in social attitudes towards children.

> 'The Convention will in all probability result in increased political attention being given to children and young people. The Convention can from now on serve

---

29 The government of the Federal Republic of Yugoslavia asked the committee to examine the violations of the rights of the children in Yugoslavia in 1993. The committee passed the case on to the Special Rapporteur on the Former Yugoslavia. See 'Federal Republic of Yugoslavia, Urgent Action requested' *International Children's Rights Monitor* 1993 vol 10 no 4 at 25.

as an "agenda" for the discussion of the actual circumstances of children'.[30]

Others disagree, for example, Vande Lanotte and Goedertier note that
'When studying the implementation mechanism of the Convention on the Rights of the Child from a judicial angle and when checking the degree to which the victim of a violation of human rights can call in the support of the Committee to cease the violation, one cannot but conclude that the control mechanism of the Convention offers only few possibilities'.[31]

Still others have agreed with Hammarberg that legal rights are not what is important: what is needed is a change in attitude, both socially and politically. The various views are not unreconcilable. One need not exclude the importance of the law as an instrument to bring about implementation of rights, while also recognising its value in bringing about social and political change.

This duality is well illustrated in the case of the UK. While there has been a change in attitudes, particularly attitudes of organisations towards children and child care, legislative changes, improvements in rights and indeed, implementation of children's rights, have also come about as a result of legal action.

The UK is a state party to the European Convention of Human Rights and has accepted the jurisdiction of the European Court on Human Rights. A number of petitions by children to the European Court seeking enforcement of their rights under the European Convention have led to fundamental legislative change and innovation in the UK. For instance, corporal punishment in schools was banned as a result of legal action

---

30 'Justice for Children through the UN Convention' in S Asquith and M Hill (eds) *Justice for Children* Dordrecht, Martinus Nijhoff 1994.
31 'The procedure before the Committee on the Rights of the Child' in E Verhellen (ed) *Understanding Children's Rights* University of Ghent 1996.

taken by a child,[32] the care system was changed after the European Court of Human Rights found the system had fundamental flaws,[33] the law on corporal punishment of children within the family is currently being reviewed following the European Court decision in *A v UK*[34] where English law was found not to have protected a child against inhuman and degrading treatment by a family member. Juvenile justice policy has also been tempered[35] and the UK is currently awaiting a decision of the Court on whether children should have the right to sue governmental child protection agencies for failure to ensure their adequate protection.[36]

3 GENERALITY OF RIGHTS

For a Convention that required for its adoption the consensus of all the participating states, many of the articles detailing rights are understandably of a very general nature. This lowest common denominator approach undoubtedly enabled more States to ratify the Convention on the Rights of the Child than might have been able otherwise to do so.

On the other hand, this approach meant that real ideological splits, as for instance on the right of the child to freedom of religion, have remained submerged. Furthermore, the desire to achieve consensus meant that it was not possible to innovate in many areas of children's rights or improve the protection offered to children, even where this was badly needed.[37] For ex-

---

32 *Campbell and Cosans v UK* 25 February 1982 Series A no 48 4 EHRR 293; *Tyrer v UK* 25 April 1978 Series A no 26 2 EHRR 1; *Costello-Roberts v UK* 25 March 1993 Series A no 247-C 19 EHRR 112.
33 Application no 25599/94, 100/1997/884/1096.
34 [1998] 2 FLR 959, EHRLR 82.
35 *R v Secretary of State for the Home Department* [1997] 3 All ER 97. See also *T and V v UK* www.dhcour.coe.fr/default.htm (report site not available at time of this publication).
36 See *X and another v Bedfordshire* [1995] AC 633. Following the decision of the House of Lords, a application was made to the European Commission on Human Rights which found the applications admissible – see Application no 29392/95 *KL and others v UK* and Application no 28945/95 *TP and KM v UK*.
37 Sweden wanted to raise the age of child soldiers.

ample, it was not possible to raise the age of recruitment into armed forces or groups to 18 years of age.

Thus, the need for active consensus allied to the generality of many provisions has resulted in a lack of protection. As Alston[38] has pointed out, this is one of the paradoxes of international human rights law. On the one hand, the norms must be sufficiently clear, comprehensive and inflexible to provide the international community with some basis on which it might seek to constrain a government which undermines or circumvents minimum standards. On the other hand, any 'universalist' convention must be characterised by a significant degree of flexibility and adaptability. Further, the generality of the rights and the need for consensus dialogue and negotiated implementation have meant that the committee have failed to interpret the rights in the Convention with any precision.

The limitations of the consensus approach with its very general statements of rights and weak enforcement mechanism are most evident in the failure to improve the rights of protection for children in situations of armed conflict.

3.1 Improving protection for children in armed conflict: the child soldier

The Report of the Special Representative for Children in Armed Conflict estimates that there are currently around 300 000 child soldiers under the age of 18 serving as combatants in government armed forces or armed opposition groups in ongoing conflicts.[39] Few states will admit to the recruitment or use of child soldiers under the age of 17 themselves, but do acknowledge that children are recruited by armed groups or forces, especially in internal armed conflicts. Such states, in their reports to the committee and as a matter of general policy, have not paid great attention to anticipating and preventing such recruitment, although they deplore the practice.

---

38 'The Best Interests Principle: Towards a reconciliation of Culture and Human Rights' in P Alston (ed) *The Best Interests of the Child, Reconciling Culture and Human Rights* at 16 Oxford, Clarendon, 1994.
39 See UN Doc A/53/482 12 October 1998 par 19.

Equally, and this is also the case for South Africa, little attention is given to the provisions of article 39 requiring programmes of rehabilitation and reintegration of such children post-conflict under the provisions of article 39.[40]

In its first report to the Committee on the Rights of the Child, South Africa briefly addresses the issue of child soldiers. The report accepts that child participation in armed forces and groups has been a big issue in Africa: the South African army recruited white boys at the age of 16, while many black children were active participants in the MK, the armed wing of the ANC.

However, the report makes no attempt to quantify the numbers of children that may have been involved, nor does it indicate what programmes have been introduced to help children reintegrate into society, or to obtain education and training to replace skills never attained or lost through early recruitment. Indeed, the only mention of provision under article 39 is restricted to the work of the Truth and Reconciliation Commission.

The lack of protection for children in armed conflict had been a matter of concern during the drafting of the Convention. It was recognised from the early stages of drafting that it would be difficult to obtain agreement from governments to extend the rights of children beyond those already offered in the Fourth Geneva Conventions and the Optional Protocols to the Geneva Conventions. Thus the age of recruitment and participation in the armed forces in article 38 of the UN Convention on the Rights of the Child remained at 15. The USA was the only state finally to refuse to agree to the proposal to raise the age to 18, but their refusal was in the end determinative, as

---

40 Article 39 provides that state parties shall take all appropriate measures to promote physical and psychological recovery and social integration of a child victim of any form of neglect, exploitation, or abuse; torture or any other form of cruel, inhuman or degrading treatment or punishment; or armed conflicts. Such recovery and reintegration shall take place in an environment which fosters the health, self-respect and dignity of the child.

all articles were adopted by consensus.[41] Those states that were at the forefront of the attempt to raise the age were reduced to entering a declaration when ratifying the convention to the effect that they took the age of recruitment and participation in the armed forces to be 18.

The issue of the age at which children should be permitted to participate in armed conflict did not disappear. The Committee on the Rights of the Child chose this topic as the subject of the first theme day of discussion. It was clear from that discussion that there was concern both in relation to continued recruitment of under-15 year olds and at the failure to use the opportunity of the drafting of the Convention to raise the age of recruitment to 18. In recognition of the limitations of the convention, further attempts have since been made to increase protection for children vulnerable to recruitment through a draft optional protocol on children involved in armed conflict (the Draft Optional Protocol to the Convention on the Rights of the Child on Involvement of Children in Armed Conflicts), through the appointment of a Special Representative for Children and Armed Conflict, and through the statutes of the International Criminal Court. The attempts to draft and agree to an optional protocol raising the level of protection for children are laudable. However, the need for an optional protocol revealed a fundamental problem with the Convention and its workings: the 'generality' of the provisions brought about by striving for consensus. The optional protocol seeks to address the need for further protection, but at the same time it ignores the basic problem of non-enforceability or implementation of the already existing provisions of the Convention.

---

41 The USA maintained this position until such time as the Convention was placed before the Commission on Human Rights, ECOSOC and the General Assembly. At this point they agreed to raising the age of recruitment and participation to 17 years of age, a position that they maintain in the latest round of negotiations on the Optional Protocol on Child Soldiers. It is somewhat ironical that the USA's non-agreement to a rise in the age from 15 to 18 during the drafting of the Convention should have been determinative as, in the event, they are one of only two states in the world which have not ratified the Convention.

The Coalition on Child Soldiers (a consortium of NGOs supporting the raising of the age of participation to 18), states and the organs of the UN, including the Committee on the Rights of the Child, have been generally unsuccessful in their efforts to assure that children under the age of 15 will not be recruited into the armed forces of states and armed groups, even though such protection is granted to them by article 38 of the Convention. Much time and effort has been given to the drafting of the optional protocol over the last four years, but still the working group has not been able to agree a finalised draft. The fifth session of the working group of the UN Commission on Human Rights, charged with the task of negotiating the optional protocol of the Convention on the Rights of the Child, opened and closed in Geneva on 11 January 1998 without agreement. Delegations agreed only that the chairperson of the working group, Ambassador Catherine von Heidenstam of Sweden, should be given another year to conduct informal consultation to determine the best way forward. Again, the need to proceed by consensus prevented an agreement being reached on an optional protocol. Once again, the USA was the major hindrance to in reaching agreement on the age of 18 for participation in armed forces, even though the USA has not itself ratified the Convention and could not, therefore, expect to be a Party to the Optional Protocol. One is faced with the inevitable conclusion that a universal consensus form of drafting may be too high a price to pay for protection of children.

The attempt to increase protection of children in armed conflict through an Optional Protocol requires real political will for any realistic change to be achieved. There is, at present, no means or mechanism for censuring states or non-state actors who utilise children in their conflicts. Nor do children have a means of securing their rights under article 38: not to be recruited or used in the army or armed group in contravention of the accepted customary international law age of 15.[42] If the pro-

---

42 But see the draft provisions of the International Criminal Court which will make the use of children as soldiers a war crime.

tection of the rights of children is to be a reality, children cannot rely on political will, which is notoriously fickle and self-interested: other mechanisms are required. The most effective means of ensuring rights, bringing about changes in law, policy and practice is through the legal enforcement of rights. It is to be regretted that pressure and campaigning for the introduction of the legal right to petition or to make a formal complaint to an appropriate court or body has not happened. The need for such measures ought to be the focus of lobbying and campaigning by international consortiums of children's NGOs to the same extent as that of raising the age for recruitment. However, such a campaign would be unlikely to achieve the financial backing or have the public appeal of a campaign to prevent child soldiers.

In advertising terms, it is not a 'sexy' issue and it would be difficult to sell as a moral crusade. In the event that the right of access to an international court to enforce rights in the Convention is unrealistic, there nevertheless needs to be a mechanism and forum where serious violations of children's rights could be aired and noted.

An obvious forum would be the Committee on the Rights of the Child. The current structure of the committee would, however, present difficulties, as the members of the committee are from different continents and states and meet only for a limited time each year. Consideration could, nonetheless, be given to the possibility of forming a small standing committee on the Rights of the Child, able to hold hearings into serious violations of children's rights, and able to raise these violations with states and non-state bodies when evidence of such is found. The pressure to cease violations would once again be moral with no sanction for refusal, other than that of world opinion.

The UN has gone some way towards providing such a body with the appointment of a Special Representative for Children and Armed Conflict. In announcing the appointment of Olarra Ottunu to this post in September 1997, the Secretary-General

'underscored the urgent need for a public advocate and moral voice on behalf of children whose rights, protection and welfare have been and are being violated in the context of armed conflict.'[43]

The Special Representative's role will be
'to ensure that the international community does not forget its obligations, encompasses not only the invocation of norms but, more important, the exertion of pressure to implement those norms and prevent the abuse and brutalisation of children.'

The Special Representative has described his role as one of public advocate for children in armed conflict, promoting concrete initiatives and mobilising a co-ordinated response to post-conflict needs. In relation to child soldiers, his role is that of mobilising public opinion and applying political pressure. In particular, he is advocating stronger and more concerted action against the military recruitment of children under the age of 15.[44] Useful though the appointment of the Special Representative has been, his tasks are enormous, encompassing both child soldiers and civilian children. His staff numbers are, however, small and the numbers of states experiencing armed conflict numerous. He is further constrained by the diplomatic requirements and niceties of the United Nations.

While he has had some notable successes in securing agreements to protect children in a number of areas, he is unlikely to have a great impact generally on the implementation of article 38 and on the prevention of recruitment of child soldiers.

A more promising initiative may prove to be the establishment of an International Criminal Court. The conscription or enlistment of children under the age of 15 years into the national armed forces or non-state armed forces or groups, or using them to participate actively in hostilities has been included in the statutes of the court as a war crime, thus criminalising specific acts of violence against children that have been, until now, purely within the category of obligations of states parties

---

43 UN Doc E/Cn 4/1998/119.
44 See UN Doc A/53/482 12 October 1998.

to international human rights treaties and international humanitarian law.[45] The establishment of a permanent International Criminal Court has not yet taken place, but is on the horizon. It is too early to know whether this will be an effective mechanism to prevent the use of young children in the armed forces, but its progress and its ability to prosecute those responsible for using children in armed forces under the age of 15 will be watched with close interest.

Another possibility is to enhance the role of the NGOs; to encourage them to take a pro-active children's rights monitoring role as well as providing mechanisms for co-operation between them, the Special Representative and the Committee on the Rights of the Child. Given the critical place of public pressure and public opinion, it is necessary to obtain credible, reliable evidence of non-implementation of children's rights.

4   CONCLUSION

Any government seeking to implement the Convention on the Rights of the Child faces a number of obstacles. These include the lack of political will to change the status of children, the lack of money available to make a real change to children's lives, the focus in a transitional society on 'adult' related matters, especially economic reform, and the public's attitude towards

---

45 Article 8 – War crimes
   1. The Court shall have jurisdiction in respect of war crimes in particular when committed as part of a plan or policy or as part of a large-scale commission of such crimes.
   2. For the purpose of this statute, 'war crimes' means:
      (a) Grave breaches of the Geneva Conventions of 12 August 1949 ...
      (b) Other serious violations of the laws and customs applicable in international armed conflict, within the established framework of international law, namely, any of the following acts: ... (xxv) Conscripting or enlisting children under the age of fifteen years into the national armed forces or using them to participate actively in hostilities ...
      (e) Other serious violations of the laws and customs applicable in armed conflicts not of an international character, within the established framework of international law, namely, any of the following acts: ... (vii) Conscripting or enlisting children under the age of fifteen years into armed forces or groups or using them to participate actively in hostilities; ...

children. While many countries postulate that in their state 'the child is King'[46] their treatment can be rather less than that accorded to royalty.

No state likes to admit that it does not give its children the best that the state has to offer. In reality, however, states frequently fail to address the major problems facing children. Children are not eligible to vote and do not constitute 'public opinion'. They have no meaningful way to object to an inadequate level of resources allocated to them by the state, whether in relation to education, health, protection or to alleviate poverty. Children are rarely granted a forum in which they can exercise a right to complain about the failure to allocate adequate resources or to have their rights implemented. Planning decisions by the state, whether economic or environmental, rarely take children's interests into account, nor consider the impact that policies are likely to have on children.

These shortcomings on the part of state parties to the Convention are exacerbated by weak monitoring, implementation and enforcement mechanisms and a failure to set minimum performance indicators or interpret rights in greater detail.

While the rate of ratification of the UN Convention on the Rights of the Child has been a triumph for the human rights world, those working in the field are well aware that there is little cause for complacency. Ratification does not carry with it an assurance that the rights contained in the Convention will be implemented. It does not translate into an improvement in the situation or status of children. Indeed, evidence from states indicates that the position of many children remains perilous and poverty-stricken. Lack of political will, a failure to change social attitudes and the lack of a legal enforcement mechanism means that for many children in the world the rights contained in the convention will remain merely aspirational. Meaningful change will not be achieved until action is taken by the international community and states to make the Convention's rights a reality.

---

46 See Dior Fall-Sow 'The Rights of Children in the African Judicial System' in E Verhellen (ed) *Understanding Children's Rights* University of Ghent 1996.

Hearing the voice of the child: notes from the Scottish experience

Lilian Edwards*

1 INTRODUCTION

How can the child be given a voice in law? This contribution will draw on the recent experience of the Scottish legal system and its attempts to implement the participation rights of the child as guaranteed by article 12 of the UN Convention on the Rights of the Child.[1] As this analysis will demonstrate, there are a number of different means by which children can be heard in law and can be enabled and encouraged to participate in both formal and informal legal processes. However the Scottish experience thus far will also demonstrate that difficulties, both theoretical and practical, arise when attempting to foreground the voice of the child by the use of law. Finally, I shall draw some general conclusions as to barriers in legal, judicial and social culture towards giving the child a voice in law and legally regulated circumstances.

Scottish family law has a degree of interest as a comparator system when considering South African child law, since Scots law, like South African law, is a mixed system, owing a great deal in origin to Roman law but with much of the modern law drawn from or influenced by contact with the English common law system. For example, as in South African law, Scots law still retains the division of children into those below the age of puberty (12 for a girl, 14 for a boy), known as pupils, and those above that age but under the age of majority, known as minors, although

---

* Senior Lecturer in Law, Edinburgh University, Scotland.
1 Adopted on 18 November 1989 and ratified by the UK on 16 December 1991.

the significance of this division has been severely reduced by recent statutory reform.[2] Clearly, however, comparisons with Scots law must be taken with caution, given the very different social, economic and cultural backgrounds to the two countries.

Until fairly recently, as in South Africa, Scottish family law was mainly to be found as part of the common law. However, since the late 1960s there has been a steady programme of statutory activity, driven by the Scottish Law Commission and particularly by the vision of one man, professor Eric Clive, which has lead to the transformation of Scots family law into that area of Scots private law which is by far the most heavily regulated by statute.

The most significant step in this quasi-codification of Scots family law thus far has been the introduction of the Children (Scotland) Act 1995, Part 1 of which deals with private law, and Part II of which deals with child protection and state intervention into child welfare (hereafter 'the 1995 Act'). One of the explicit and leading goals underlying the 1995 Act was the desire to bring Scots law into compliance with the UN Convention on the Rights of the Child and especially with article 12 which deals with the rights of children to participate (see United Nations International Convention on the Rights of the Child, page 135). The White Paper Scotland's Children[3] which tested the ground for the Children Act, for example, cited the UN Convention on the Rights of the Child as 'one of the driving forces behind the desire to empower children' and demanded that 'the views of children should always be taken seriously and given due weight in reaching decisions'. As will be explored below, there were a number of areas of Scots law before the 1995 Act where there was serious concern that the challenge posed by article 12 was not met.

Almost all the states in the world (191 at date of writing, including South Africa and the United Kingdom) have signed the UN Convention on the Rights of the Child. It can thus be asserted that it represents, in ideal if not necessarily in practice, the mini-

---

2 See the Age of Legal Capacity (Scotland) Act 1991.
3 Cm 2286 (1993).

mum standard of participation which states must guarantee to the child. How is this standard implemented in Scots law?

For the purpose of this book, it is useful to identify two different ways in which children can be allowed, in the words of the UN Convention, to 'express their views freely' in matters that affect them.

> **1) Participation.** This term will be used to cover all rules which allow the voice of the child to be heard directly, without intermediary. This includes rules that demand that children be consulted about their opinion, or which enable children to become parties to legal actions, so that they have the right to interact with the proceedings and/or to demand a certain legal remedy.
>
> **2) Representation.** This term will be used to discuss rules which allow children and young persons to instruct solicitors, seek legal advice or have other kinds of adult representation in various types of legal or quasi-legal proceedings.

2 PARTICIPATION

The Children (Scotland) Act 1995 contains three key provisions relating to the right of the child to be consulted.

2.1 Sections 11(7) and 16 of the 1995 Act

The first provision to be considered, in section 11(7) of the Act, is concerned exclusively with court orders relating to parental responsibilities and rights. The significance of this section needs a little explanation. The Children (Scotland) Act, in line with legislation in other countries, including, notably, the Children Act 1989 in England, attempts to reform the relationship between parent and child by abolishing the common law concepts of rights of custody and access. The award of sole custody by a court, usually made in most divorces to the mother, was seen at common law as conferring the right to run most areas of the child's life, leading to the effective exclusion of the noncustodial parent from the child's life after divorce. The 1995 Act seeks to replace this with a childcentred model where both parents (if married) are encouraged to play a continuing role in the child's life even after divorce. Parents are seen as owing responsibilities **to** the child rather than having rights **over** the child, with a presumption that this joint responsibility will continue after divorce unless there is good reason to alter it by court order.[4] Parental rights still exist, but are expressly stated to be given to parents only for the fulfilment of parental responsibilities and to be exercised in the best interests of the child.[5]

The heart of these new rules relating to children, parents and separation and divorce is to be found in section 11. Instead of seeking an order for custody or access, parents can now only seek one or more of a number of specialised but flexible orders.

For example, a residence order can be sought which regulates the arrangements for where a child under 16 is to live. A contact order regulates the arrangements for maintaining personal relations with such a child.

A 'specific issue' order can be made which regulates any specific issue relating to parental responsibility, such as how the child should be educated, in what religion he or she should be raised or whether he or she should be allowed to receive a certain medical treatment. Finally an order can be sought from the court to deprive any other person of aspects of parental rights or responsibilities. These orders are thus the principal means by which the courts regulate the living arrangements for children where these are disputed in the wake of divorce or other types of interfamily conflict.

How is the voice of the child dealt with in section 11? The court in considering whether to make a section 11 order must have regard to three overarching principles.[6] First, the welfare of the child is its paramount consideration. Secondly, the court should not make any order unless it considers it better to do so than to make none at all (the so-called 'minimum intervention'

---

4   S 11(7)(a) of the 1995 Act.
5   S 2 (1).
6   S 11(7).

principle.) Thirdly, (and most importantly for the current discussion) the court shall, taking account of the child's age and maturity, give the child an opportunity to indicate whether he or she wishes to express a view; and if such a wish is expressed, then an opportunity to express views must be given; and finally, the court must then give due regard to such views as may be expressed.[7]

There is a similar provision to section 11(7) in section 16 of the Act in relation to the child protection and state intervention provisions of Part II of the 1995 Act. Thus if a court or a children's hearing[8] is making an order to, for example, remove a child from home, exclude an alleged abuser from the home or place the child under social work supervision, then again the same rule of consultation will apply. Most of what is said below applies to both but in the main we will concentrate on the private law provisions of section 11(7).

Section 11(7) and section 16 are clearly intended formally to meet the demands of article 12 of the UN Convention. However it is of little use to give children formal rights of consultation when their parents divorce if there is no way they can **in practice** get their views heard. Prior to the 1995 Act, case law suggested that judges also habitually had regard for the views of children, when they were presented, although these views were subordinate (as under the 1995 Act) to the paramountcy of the welfare principle.

As it was put in the pre-1995 Act Scottish case of *Fowler v Fowler*,[9] 'it cannot be assumed that a child's interests necessarily coincide with her wishes'. However, effectively no satisfactory procedure existed to allow children an opportunity to get those views into the court, rendering this principle something

---

7 S 11(10) further states that a child of 12 or over shall be **presumed** to be of sufficient age and maturity to form a view for these purposes.

8 In Scotland, children can be referred to a children's hearing if they meet certain grounds of referral; basically, if they have committed offences, have been the victim of an offence, or are otherwise seen as in need of care and protection. The hearing is a lay body, but its decisions can be appealed to the courts, as can the grounds of referral. See further chapter 8 of L Edwards and A Griffiths *Family Law* W Green, Sweet & Maxwell 1997.

9 1981 SLT (Notes) 9.

of a dead letter from the point of view of child participation rights. Scottish divorce actions (where most disputes relating to parental rights and responsibilities did, and still do, arise) were procedurally constructed as disputes between the parents, where children were discussed by the adults, rather than involved as parties. Scottish divorce procedure allows disputes to be settled by the submission of documentary evidence (known as affidavits) and only some 2% of divorces involve the hearing of oral evidence, let alone the oral evidence of children.[10] The overwhelming majority of divorces (some 80% in 1991) are in any case undefended, in which case the court only has to satisfy itself that adequate arrangements have been made for the children.[11] This duty could be satisfied prior to the 1995 Act merely by receiving satisfactory affidavits from the pursuer and one other witness, who might be a friend or relative or other connected person, and without seeing or hearing from the child directly by any means whatsoever.

In practice, this meant that the court was thus almost always appraised of the views of the child, if at all, only through an adult and partisan filter. In some, invariably disputed, cases, the court *might* choose to order that an independent report on child care arrangements be compiled by a social worker, solicitor or advocate, but these cases were relatively exceptional, and furthermore it would still usually be at the discretion of the appointed reporter if they chose to speak directly to the child, or merely to the adults concerned. Most damning of all, a child might not even know that his or her parents were divorcing and arguing over where, say, he or she would live in future.

Since the child was not an automatic party to divorce proceedings, no intimation or details of legal proceedings would be sent to that child. The first time the child might learn that the court had been deciding about his or her future, might be after the custody order had already been awarded.

---

10 This and other statistics substantially drawn from Morris, Gibson and Platts *Untying the Knot* Scottish Office Central Research Unit Papers, 1993.
11 This rule is now found in s 12 of the 1995 Act, but existed under the prior law as well.

These rules were extensively criticised during the consultation period of the 1995 Act as failing to adhere to the standards of article 12, and as a result the Scottish rules of court governing procedure in family actions were reformed in 1996.[12] As a first step, the new rules demand that in any family action affecting a child, that child is to receive intimation of the action via a form known as the 'F9 form'. This is sent through the post by recorded delivery.

In order to prevent the child receiving full particulars of the action, which might, it was thought, contain potentially distressing accounts of marital behaviour, the pursuer's solicitor is instructed to give a summary on the form of what the action is about, in language which 'a child is capable of understanding'. The form then invites the child to inform the sheriff[13] if he or she has something to say about the proceedings. This can be done either by returning the F9 form, or by writing a separate letter to the court. The child is offered two options on the form: first, of speaking to the court via a third party the child names (and the suggestion is made of a friend, relative or teacher but, notably, not a parent); or secondly, of writing to the sheriff direct with his or her views.

The sheriff can then choose to take whatever steps he or she feels necessary to ascertain the views of the child, including speaking directly to the child, in open court, or in private in chambers.

The F9 form is a clear improvement over the old law, where children were offered almost no opportunity to get a say in divorce proceedings, but it is clear that it is still rife with inadequacies. There are three basic sets of problems.

(i) The form itself. Since it is posted to the child's address, and many children share their home with one or both parents, there is no guarantee the child will ever even receive it. Anecdotes abound of parents opening the form and throwing it away so that the child never sees it. Parents may feel threatened by the

---

12 Act of Sederunt (Family Proceedings in the Sheriff Court)1996 SI 1996 no 2167.
13 The first instance judge in civil proceedings in Scotland is known as a sheriff.

concept of their children being given the chance to speak in court[14] or may fail to understand the significance of the form. Even if the child receives the form, literacy levels may not allow the child to understand it without assistance, and it seems uncontroversial to state that without special training, solicitors are not the right people to write anything down in supposedly 'child-friendly' language. No additional information is available to the child other than the bare form, and there is no easily accessible person to explain what it all means.[15] Informal research by the Scottish Child Law Centre found that comprehension levels of children handed F9 forms were low and reactions negative. The form was described as 'scary' and 'intimidating' – 'something to do with abused children' said one child shown the draft form.[16]

(ii) Will the child have a meaningful opportunity to communicate his or her views, even if he or she manages to return the form or otherwise communicate the fact that he or she wishes to speak to the sheriff? Speaking to a sheriff in court is a worrying experience for most adults let alone for many children, especially those from a country such as Scotland where children are often relatively inarticulate and unassertive, especially under stressful circumstances. Although some sheriffs have an interest in receiving the views of children and have been successful at it, many have neither the aptitude nor the training to deal with children in the artificial and intimidating environment of a court. Sheriffs receive no special training in child interview techniques or psychology at present, which is all the more unfortunate given that many other specialists such as child social workers now do. As one experienced family lawyer put it:

---

14 See R Gallacher *Children and Young People's Voices on the Law, Legal Services and Systems In Scotland* published by the Scottish Child Law Centre, Cranston House, 108 Argyle St, Glasgow, G2 8BH, March 1998, hereafter referred to as 'Gallacher' at 68.
15 The form does give notice of a free advice telephone line for children set up by the Scottish Child Law Centre. However the SCLC itself reports that very little use has been made of this in relation to F9 form intimation.
16 SCLC response to Consultation by Sheriff Court Rules Council on Part I of the Children (Sc) Act 1995, July 1996.

> 'It is a matter of happy accident if the sheriff has got any real skill at talking to a child. There are a lot about on the bench who conspicuously don't have the skills for talking to anybody, far less a child...'[17]

The difference in age, class and circumstances between children and judges also may inhibit communication. As another family lawyer commented:

> 'A lot of sheriffs interview children and then come out and say they don't know why they did that, as they were no further forward than they were before. It has to be said however, that if a child from a working class background is being interviewed by some guy with a posh accent, he might as well be on the moon.'[18]

Most sheriffs will interview children in their chambers, perhaps with wig and gown removed to be less intimidating, but some insist that the child be interviewed in the body of the court, in the interests of fair play to the other parties to the action, as the child's evidence may prove decisive to the decision at the end of the day. As one sheriff put it:

> 'While I think it's right that the children's views should be regarded as sacrosanct and privileged, on the other hand I think it's unfair on the parties because I'm making a decision based on information which neither of them has seen ... So you're balancing ... the protection of the children against the natural justice owing to the parties and I think that's an irreconcilable quandary.'[19]

(iii) If children do manage to make their views known, will they be guaranteed confidentiality? As seen above, sheriffs are troubled by the implications of hearing children give oral evidence in private as opposed to open court. This problem also

---

17 Gallacher at 63.
18 Gallacher at 63.
19 *Evaluation of Mediation in Family Disputes in Scotland* Scottish Office Central Research Unit Report, forthcoming 1999.

extends to any other views expressed by the child by whatever means. The new Scottish rules of court state that if a child does choose to express views, orally or in writing to the sheriff, then the sheriff **must** record the views expressed in writing within the court process.[20] Normally this record will then be sealed as confidential, and kept in the file in a special envelope. However the sheriff has a discretion to reveal what the child has said to the other parties, for example, in the interests of natural justice. Given that children are often reluctant in any case to be seen as favouring one parent over another, the lack of guaranteed confidentiality when views are expressed about parenting choices may be a powerful disincentive to the expression of any opinion at all. Yet in the current system, those determining if confidentiality should be preserved – sheriffs – by nature of their habitual work in adversarial and, especially, criminal proceedings, tend to put a lower value on the child's privacy than on procedural justice. One sheriff indeed has said that 'I think it's actually patronising towards children – you tell us this, we won't tell anybody.'[21]

Are there any solutions to these problems? In consultation prior to the introduction of the new rules, both the Scottish Child Law Centre and Children in Scotland denounced the postal intimation scheme as inadequate and perplexing. Their preferred option was that in every case involving a child of sufficient maturity, a child advocate or representative should be appointed who could explain the action to the child, receive views and possibly convey them to the court. These suggestions were however rejected, principally, it appears on cost grounds, a point explored further below in relation to representation.

---

20 Act of Sederunt (Family Proceedings in the Sheriff Court) 1996 r 33.20.
21 *Evaluation of Mediation in Family Disputes in Scotland* Scottish Office Central Research Unit Report, forthcoming 1999 at 91, and see also quotes by children at Gallacher 32 on the importance they attached to confidentiality.

2.2 Section 6 of the 1995 Act

The second major provision in the 1995 Act affecting children's rights to participation is section 6. The rule of consultation in section 11(7) does allow for a degree of participation by children in court proceedings in theory, even if the implementation is extremely flawed. But of course not all decisions of importance to a child will be made in, or challenged in, legal proceedings. In the overwhelming majority of Scottish divorces, residence and contact issues are now entirely negotiated privately between the parties rather than disputed in court. Studies of the solicitor's role in divorce in Scotland have repeatedly shown that lawyers promote negotiated, consensual settlements and view the resolution of disputes via argument in court as a last resort.[22] As noted above, as a result, around 80% of divorces involving children are undefended. In such cases parties will almost always have resolved child care issues themselves, either with or without the help of solicitors in negotiation. Furthermore, some 20% of Scottish divorces involving children, also involve a formal written minute of agreement made by the parents about issues such as child care and property, which is almost invariably rubber stamped by the court without further investigation.[23]

This degree of consensus that child care arrangements are better settled out of court may be a peculiarly Scottish phenomenon. But parents in many countries are also increasingly directed towards non-legal forums such as mediation or conciliation services to reach agreements about child care – not least because these are regarded as cheaper in terms of the state's legal aid burden than court proceedings, but also because there is a prevalent assumption that a non-adversarial forum is a better venue for reaching decisions about family breakdown than

---

22 See Wasoff, Dobash and Harcus *The Impact of the Family Law (Sc) Act 1985 on Solicitor's Divorce Practice* Scottish Office, CRU Report, 1990; Wasoff, McGucken and Edwards *Mutual Consent: Written Agreements in Family Law* Scottish Office Central Research Unit Report,1997; *Evaluation of Mediation in Family Disputes in Scotland*, Scottish Office Central Research Unit Report, forthcoming 1999.

23 See further Wasoff, McGucken and Edwards *Mutual Consent: Written Agreements in Family Law* Scottish Office Central Research Unit Report,1997.

a formal, adversarial court. Scotland has not yet reached the same level of institutionalised support for mediation as England, where at least one session of mediation is effectively compulsory before legal aid can be obtained,[24] but it does have an increasing culture of referral to mediation from the courts or by solicitors. Yet although one of the ostensible goals of mediation is to further the child's best interests, in practice children are not usually party to mediation sessions. Parents in fact often see mediation as a private space where they can say what they really think without their children being hurt.

Mediators also tend to feel that children should not be placed in the position of being caught in domestic conflict and, in particular, forced openly to choose between one parent and another. As Martin Richards has pointed out, this is all very well but where does it leave the voice of the child?[25] It seems paradoxical that at the time when strenuous efforts are being made to give children a voice in formal legal proceedings, child care disputes are increasingly being shifted towards non-formal arenas such as mediation, where safeguards to allow the child a voice are largely absent.

In such circumstances, how can a child persuade parents (or other significant adults), rather than a court, to hear and give weight to their wishes and feelings? Section 6 of the 1995 Act attempts to deal with this issue. It provides that:

'A person shall, in reaching any major decision which involves –
- (a) his fulfilling a parental responsibility ; or
- (b) his exercising a parental right or giving consent by virtue of that section, have regard so far as practicable to the views (if he wishes to express them) of the child concerned, taking account of the child's age and maturity ... ; a child 12 years of age or more shall be presumed to be of sufficient age and maturity to express a view.'

---

[24] Family Law Act 1996.
[25] 'But What About the Children? Some Reflections on the Divorce White Paper' (1995) 7 *Canadian Fam Law Quarterly* 223.

Following section 6, a parent should in theory, when negotiating on (say) contact arrangements, consult the sufficiently mature child who will be affected by them. But this raises a host of questions. The most crucial and obvious is that such 'private sphere' provisions are inherently unenforceable. Even the Scottish Law Commission has admitted that section 6 is largely exhortatory,[26] and cannot be monitored or enforced without drastic invasions of family privacy. Furthermore the section 6 obligation applies only to persons exercising parental responsibilities or rights. Thus in the mediation scenario described above, parents have a duty to consult their children – but mediators do not.

Looking beyond divorce, section 6 clearly has very wide applicability. It should mean that children should be consulted about where the family lives, what religious practices are followed and what types of discipline are inflicted. There is however an enormous credibility gap between law and actuality which it is difficult to see narrowing.

2.3 General problems relating to participation in the 1995 Act

If we move from the detailed analysis of the problems of implementing section 11 and section 6 to a more general assessment of the 1995 Act provisions, another overriding problem appears. The provisions cover only a tiny fraction of legal events affecting children. There are no entrenched rights of consultation for children in vital public law areas such as labour law, education law, welfare benefits law or housing and homelessness rights. Even within the family law area, children do not have to be consulted in matters crucially affecting them such as proceedings to exclude their father from the home for domestic violence,[27] or in applications for child support,[28] or in child abduc-

---

26 See SLC *Report on Family Law* Scottish Law Commission No 135 (May 1992) paras 2.60-2.66.
27 See the Matrimonial Homes (Family Proceedings) (Sc) Act 1981.
28 See the Child Support Act 1991.

tion proceedings under the Hague Convention on the Civil Aspects of International Child Abduction.[29] Children may have a voice if they themselves instruct proceedings or seek to be joined as parties to proceedings, of course (explored further below), but they are only **automatically** parties to criminal proceedings where they are the accused, and where they come before the children's hearings system, which deals with children in need of compulsory measures of supervision.[30] Again therefore the problem arises that children may not even know of proceedings raised by adults affecting their vital interests. The child's voice, outside the small fields of private law parental responsibilities actions and public law child protection proceedings, is thus noticeable mainly by its absence.

3 REPRESENTATION

The right of legal representation is inherently crucial for the implementation of the voice of the child. As seen above, article 12 (2) of the UN Convention explicitly recognises that the child may express a view directly or via a representative. Children by their very nature are often unable to speak on their own behalf in legal proceedings. They may simply be too young to speak, too unskilled in oral presentation or too intimidated by a courtroom atmosphere or by the presence of their parents, particularly in actions taken against one or both parents. In some cases professional practice rules will demand that a party is represented by legal counsel rather than speaks for him or herself. Outside the courtroom, access to legal advice and representation is essential if children are fully to take advantage of the

---

29 See the Child Abduction and Custody Act 1985 for UK implementation. Under the Hague Convention, it *is* an argument that an abducted child should not be returned to their state of habitual residence that the child of sufficient age and maturity objects to his or her return (art 13 Hague Convention); however UK courts are inclined to use this exception to the general duty of return sparingly – see *Urness v Minto* 1994 SLT 988, where child's objections were accepted cf *Marshall v Marshall* 1996 SLT 429.
30 Supra n 8.

remedies provided by the legal system and are to be able to negotiate on a level playing field with other agents who are legally represented. It is essential to look not just at the rules which theoretically regulate a child's right to representation, and the difficulties surrounding them, but at practical hurdles such as access to financial assistance and judicial attitudes.

The representation of children is an area which in Scotland has a mixed and confusing history.[31] There are essentially two types of persons loosely referred to as a child's representative – those whose job it is to represent what is in the child's best interests ('welfare representatives') and those who, like solicitors, are professionally required to act for their client according to the client's wishes ('true' representatives). As in the current South African system, before the 1995 Act, Scottish children under the age of majority had no rights to litigate without the assistance of their parent or guardian, unless no such person existed, or there was a conflict between the child and the parent, in which case a curator *ad litem* might be appointed by the court to act for the child. The curator was, and is, however, not a true representative of the child's wishes, but rather an officer of the court whose job is to determine what is in the child's best interests – a welfare representative. A similar officer can be appointed by the children's hearing or a court in child protection cases, and is then known as a safeguarder[32] – a revealing name since they safeguard the child's interests rather than represent his or her wishes. In 1991, the age of legal capacity was reduced to 16 in Scotland,[33] but it was left uncertain what rights, if any, children under 16 had to litigate without the consent of their parents in civil matters. Where a child of any age over the limit of criminal responsibility (8 years old in Scotland) was accused of a crime, however, it had always been recognised that the child could instruct his or her defence counsel.

---

31 See further A Cleland 'The Child's Right to be Represented in Legal Proceedings', chapter 4 of A Cleland and E Sutherland (eds) *Children's Rights in Scotland* W Green 1996.
32 S 41(1) 1995 Act.
33 Age of Legal Capacity (Sc) Act 1991.

Thus when the 1995 Act was going through parliament, it was realised that reform was necessary if the demands of article 12 were to be met , that a child, like an adult, should have an opportunity to have his or her **wishes** rather than his or her **interests** presented by a legal representative of his or her own choosing. Accordingly a late amendment was made to the Act[34] which provides that:
(a) children under 16 can instruct solicitors in civil matters so long as they have a general understanding of what it means to do so (such competence being presumed at age 12); and
(b) a person who has such legal capacity then **also** has capacity to bring or defend civil proceedings.

As with the intimation rules discussed above, on paper this looks good. The provision applies in relation to **any** civil proceedings, not just family actions, for example, and in that respect is wider than the parallel English provisions[35] – this appears however to have been a drafting error rather than a deliberate attempt to empower children.[36] The actuality however again leaves something to be desired. For one thing, whose job is it to decide if the child has a general understanding? The court? The solicitor whom the child seeks to instruct? The child's parents? The matter is left silent. So far, the anecdotal evidence from Scotland is that solicitors have *de facto* taken on the role of assessment, without challenge from the courts, although what criteria solicitors are using remains opaque. It is again not unlikely that some or most solicitors will lack extensive knowledge, of the developmental stages in children's maturity or knowledge and in the Gallacher survey[37] many expressed dubiety at their ability to communicate fully with children.[38] In England, despite a more clearly drafted provision which indicates that the solicitor has a role to assess competence, in many cases this role

---

34 1995 Act, Sched 4 par 53, substituting into the Age of Legal Capacity (Sc) Act 1991, new ss 2(4A) and (4B).
35 S 10(8) Children Act 1989 and r 4.7 Family Proceedings Rules 1991 (SI 1991 no 1247).
36 Private conversation with Scottish Office by PhD student.
37 At 63.
38 Gallacher at 64-65.

has been usurped by the courts[39] which have repeatedly invoked protective welfare criteria to exclude children from representation in actions, even after solicitors had assessed the children as competent.[40] The courts have seemed willing to subordinate the right of a child to a voice to the need to protect the child from, for example, exposure to potentially upsetting evidence – even though it might be thought that a child must be unusually resilient to have gone so far as to take the unusual course of seeking independent representation.

It is clearly a problem for both judges and solicitors, not aided by ambiguous legislation, to decide if the child's right to participate is an absolute one; or one which should be balanced against protective criteria; or one which is always subordinate to the child's welfare. Their training has not in general prepared them to know what role they should play in relation to children and it is unsurprising and perhaps inevitable that the paternalistic attitudes embedded in the system persist. The representatives themselves may find their role confusing and compromised by concerns for the child's welfare and conflicts may arise between different types of representatives acting for the child in a single attitude. Some interesting evidence on this point has been collected. Gallacher[41] asked a sample of 46 solicitors who had acted for child clients how they saw their role. 'Officially' of course, the role of a solicitor is to take instructions from the child and to represent the child's wishes; the court should appoint a curator *ad litem* if it wishes a welfare representative to be present. In fact Gallacher found that, only 16 of the solicitors questioned said they would 'usually' act according to the child's instructions; while 21 said they would usually or sometimes act according to the child's interests instead. It seems questionable from this if solicitors are giving the same kind of service to their child clients as to adults. Some solicitors also reported to Gallacher disbelief that children knew what they wanted, while others reported ethical conflict when they perceived children

---

39 The leading case is *Re T (A Minor) (Wardship: Representation)* [1993] 2 FLR 278.
40 See eg *Re S (A Minor) (Wardship: Representation)* [1993] 2 FLR 437.
41 At 63.

as putting themselves in unfortunate situations like entering into conflict with strongly held opinions by parents.[42]

Judicial attitudes may also be affected by paternalistic notions embedded historically in the legal system. In a recent Scottish case, *Henderson v Henderson*,[43] a girl of ten instructed a solicitor so that she could be joined as a party to her parents' dispute over whether the father should have contact. The girl agreed with her mother that she did not wish to see her father in future, but she also wanted the right to make that statement herself in court. The sheriff made the following comments:

> 'I do not regard the fact that the child entered the process as a party as of assistance. It is difficult to see what advantage [this] has in a situation where the child's views are exactly the same as the defenders. I can see there might be some advantage if the child had views that were different from the views of both the other parties, but otherwise it appears an unnecessary complication. ... As all three parties were also on legal aid, it also appears an unnecessary expense! ... The court should normally be able to have regard to the views of the child without the child entering the process and while there may always be exceptional cases, I would deprecate any general tendency for applications to be made for children to be party.'

There are clearly many important points raised by these kind of statements. It might be suggested that the point of article 12 is to allow children to participate in legal proceedings merely so their wishes can be voiced where they might not otherwise come to light – where there is, for example, conflict between what the child in quesion wants, and what (say) parents, doctors or social workers want for that child.

If that is what article 12 is really about, then the judge in *Henderson* is correct when he says that a curator *ad litem* or a

---

42 Gallacher at 67-69.
43 1997 Fam LR 120.

court reporter (or a parent) may suffice to report what the child wants, and that anything more is redundant. On the other hand, another interpretation of article 12 is that it is designed to empower children, by allowing them to participate as adults do, by according them respect for their autonomy, and by treating them as equals in the proceeding, not, in the famous phrase, merely as 'objects of concern'.[44]

Finally, the *Henderson* judgment raises the spectre of money. It does seem to indicate a rather empty commitment to children's rights if we are willing to give them a voice but only where it does not cost the state any money. When the rights of independent litigation for children described above were introduced, the Scottish Legal Aid Board (SLAB) also indicated they would accept applications from children for civil legal aid and legal advice and assistance funding, so long as the solicitor instructed certified that the child was sufficiently competent.[45]

As a result, the number of applications from children for legal aid doubled in the first year of the new rules, although it still represents in total only 3% of total civil legal aid applications. However there is preliminary evidence that only about two-thirds of applications by children are being granted by SLAB.[46] Given that most children will have no or little income, there must be some non-finance related reason why these applications are being refused. There is some evidence from SLAB guidelines that applications are being refused on the basis that the child has 'no need of separate representation' – because, for example, the child's views are also shared by a parent litigant (as in *Henderson*), or the child's views, it is felt, can be adequately represented by a court reporter, or by affidavit. It seems then, that there is some danger that although the state may be willing to allow the child a voice in principle, it is unwilling to back it with adequate public funding.

---

44 The Hon Mrs Justice Butler-Sloss *Report into the Inquiry into Child Abuse in Cleveland* Cm 412 1987.
45 See (1996) *Journal of the Law Society of Scotland* 83.
46 Figures from unpublished research for the Scottish Office, F Kean 'Research into the Uptake of Civil Legal Aid by Children Under 16 and its Implications for Solicitors' 1997.

4 CONCLUSIONS

Having analysed and critiqued in detail the means by which the Scottish system attempts to implement the voice of the child, it is now possible to draw some more general concluding thoughts. First, it is apparent that the Scots system is incoherent, and has arisen as a result of piecemeal concern, and historical accident. As we have seen, there is careful regulation of the child's right to participate within the limited framework of the 1995 Act, but no parallel concern in the public law sphere, or even throughout the rest of family law legislation. There are no provisions demanding that children be given an opportunity to speak when their parents are accessing welfare or housing rights, or seeking child support, even though the child may be profoundly affected by the results. On the other hand, there are a few occasions in the legal system where the child's voice is not only heard but is **decisive**. A child can, for example, veto his or her own adoption in Scotland from the age of 12,[47] or refuse to submit to medical assessment for evidence of abuse if he or she is adjudged to have reached a standard of sufficient age and maturity.[48] Why is it so important that children must have a final say in these areas, but not about, for example, where they should live? Bodily integrity is important of course, but so is the right to choose a home. In a system intending to codify its child law, as South Africa is,[49] these issues should be thought through, not be determined, as they have been in Scotland, by historic accident and short-term concerns. It is also incoherent, as we have seen above, who **decides** if the child can participate in legal decisions – should it be the judge? Parents? Mediators? Solicitors? Legal aid boards?

Secondly, it is trite but necessary to observe that there is a clear tension between the participation and the protection of children. Judges, as noted above, are often unhappy at the pros-

---

47 Adoption (Scotland) Act 1978, s 12(8).
48 S 90 of the 1995 Act and s 2(4) of the Age of Legal Capacity (Sc) Act 1991.
49 South African Law Commission, Issue Paper 13, Project 110, *The Review of the Child Care Act*, First Issue Paper (April 1998).

pect of seeing children in court and may feel that the best thing from a welfare point of view to do is to keep them well away from a potentially hurtful and damaging adult process. These protective instincts may be reinforced by the fact that they themselves are more comfortable dealing with adults such as court reporters and curators *ad litem* than with children direct, unsurprising when they have no training themselves in child communication.[50]

Mediators are often unhappy about seeing children for similar reasons (although they may well have better skills at communication than sheriffs), and parents in divorce actions may also wish to keep their children out of the firing line in what they see as a fight between themselves and the ex partner.

Although the instinct to exclude the voice of the child may be paternalistic, it also sometimes expresses correct and deeply held concern for the child's welfare. It is trite psychology that children feel responsible for their actions when asked, for example, to pick between one parent and the other, and that they may not wish to be placed in those kind of positions of adult responsibility. Again however there is some evidence that children themselves are less sensitive souls than some adults suppose, and deeply resent being excluded from adult legal processes.

Children have probably been aware of family breakdown for a long time before it ends up in the courts and may already know most of the details. Some of the children in Gallacher's survey deeply resented the fact that they were never asked what **they** wanted when their parents were divorcing.[51] Those implementing the voice of the child cannot simply assume that all children of whatever age and maturity are too fragile to engage with the law.

Thirdly, there are again clear and obvious tensions between the autonomy of children and the autonomy of parents. Allowing the child a voice may be seen as a challenge to the power or autonomy of the family or adults concerned – Gallacher reports

---
50 See Gallacher at 62-64.
51 Gallacher at 35.

one experienced family law practitioner thus on separate representation of children:

> 'In most scenarios where there is a conflict between the parent and child, what they don't want is for the child to be in any position of power, or in any position to contradict what they say. It's easy to be powerful and manipulative, adult-to-child – but the minute you bring in another adult to act for the child it strengthens the child's position, and the parents don't like it.'[52]

Adults are used to infringing child autonomy. Have we yet reached the stage where as the logical end product of giving the child a voice we are willing to contemplate the child infringing adult autonomy? What will we do, for example, when children consistently say, as studies show they will, that in fact what they would really like is for their parents not to split up at all? Would we rather the law really paid lip service to article 12 than actually grappled with implementing it in a meaningful fashion?

Fourthly, there are financial tensions about implementing the voice of the child. The straight questions is, are we willing to put our money where the child's mouth is? As we have seen above, there are difficult issues here in relation to who pays for child advocacy, how to deal with multiple possible representatives (in English care proceedings it is not at all uncommon for a child to be represented by a guardian *ad litem* as well as having separate representation, all on legal aid) and access to legal aid. It is easy and cheap to implement something like the F9 form scheme but how useful is the end product? A connected point is that it is of little use to give children formal rights of participation, however marvellous, if they do not **know** about them.

Education about rights also costs money. Gallacher found from questionnaires that around a third of her sample (of 213 children) claimed they already knew 'enough' about divorce,

---

52 Gallacher at 68.

residence and contact issues and only 24 thought it was 'very important' for them to know more. However, when queried further, she discovered that virtually none of these children was aware of his or her rights under the 1995 Act to be consulted and to instruct solicitors.[53] Similarly, virtually none had heard of the UN Convention on the Rights of the Child.[54] This would seem to imply a pressing need to spend money on public rights education, perhaps via the school curriculum, if children are realistically to deploy their rights. The Scottish Child Law Centre has suggested that teaching packs on children's rights be distributed to schools and has co-operated with the Scottish Office in producing a glossy photo-comic style brochure called 'You Matter' which has been widely distributed to solicitors, parents, and so on in a bid to give children an accessible source of information about their rights under the 1995 Act. Another approach sometimes mooted is the appointment of a Children's Rights Commissioner whose ambit might include everything from high-profiling children's rights to taking on leading test cases.[55]

But before we get too carried away with schemes to publicise children's rights, we also need to face the fact that hard choices may have to be made as to which of children's rights should be implemented, given limited global resources. Is the voice of the child the most important item on the agenda? Is the UN Convention a holistic text which can only be implemented as a whole or not at all? It is noticeable that the South African Constitution protects the welfare and protection interests of children in a style very similar to the UN Convention, but does not entrench the right of children to participate.[56]

This may recognise correctly that at present in South Africa welfare needs to be placed above participation in terms of resources, given the standard of living of many of South Africa's

---

53 Gallacher at 15.
54 Gallacher at 36.
55 See Rosenbaum and Newell *Taking Children Seriously* (1991). Gallacher endorses this call (38).
56 S 28 of the 1996 Constitution.

children. On the other hand it can be argued that it is crucial for South Africa's children to be given and made aware of their civil rights if they are to understand and constitute a democratic society in the future.

Fifthly, finally, and perhaps most controversially, we need to consider if the child's voice is best furthered by participation and representation in **legal** processes at all. As a society and as signatories to the UN Convention, we are concerned to provide children with access to legal representation, yet studies show that in fact children distrust and feel alienated from lawyers and law centres, and overwhelmingly turn to their parents as their first port of call for help and advice. In Gallacher's study, children were extraordinarily negative about contact with solicitors. Lawyers were described as unapproachable, rich, wearing suits and ties, and too important to waste their time on children. They spoke impenetrable jargon and charged huge fees. One quote sums up the sense of total disempowerment felt by children who came into contact with lawyers:

> 'I remember my mum going to a lawyer and I was terrified by him. There was this big intimidating building. I was intimidated all the way through with this giant desk. I felt so uncomfortable because I was sitting behind this big massive desk and that was all I could see.'[57]

Unsurprisingly only 8 out of 213 in Gallacher's sample had ever asked a solicitor for advice.[58]

The response from the children's rights community has often been to suggest that the law must be made more approachable by children. A specialism in child law for solicitors, perhaps with added communication and psychological skills, can be developed. Specialist child practices can be set up (one has been, apparently successfully, in Edinburgh). Law centres can be located in deprived areas with less than ostentatious facades to play a role, as can children's rights centres, helplines and

---

57 Gallacher at 21.
58 Gallacher at 18.

hotlines. This is all valuable work. But it should perhaps also be asked if we should not also be looking at ways of allowing the child a voice other than through an expensive, upsetting and problematic legal process. Perhaps we need to return to the challenge of public education, but with a remit to encourage participatory democracy within the family, as section 6 seeks to do in its own way, rather than regarding the family as the natural enemy of the child's voice.[59]

Perhaps we need to encourage children to play a role themselves in the creation of laws from the beginning, as has been done in Slovenia,[60] or at least to make sure our laws are 'child-proofed' from the start. In Scotland, there is now a ministerial commitment to ensuring that all new legislation complies with the demands of the UN Convention,[61] but this still does not mean that children are actually involved in the planning or drafting stages of Bills. Perhaps, finally, what we need to consider is whether respect for the voice of the child arises from respect for the child as a human being in all areas of life, not just those mediated by law and legal processes. That is the real challenge involved in implementing article 12.

---

59 Gallacher found that children were more likely to turn to parents for advice than to anyone else but friends – and considerably more likely to consult parents rather than youth workers, solicitors, law centres or childrens' rights officers (18).
60 Z Pavlovic 'Children's Parliament in Slovenia' in M John (ed) *Children in Charge: The Child's Right to a Fair Hearing* Jessica Kingsley 1996.
61 Scottish Office Child Strategy Statement, available at http://www.scotland.gov.uk/frame21.htm.

From parents' rights to children's rights

June Sinclair*

In 1994, in a piece entitled 'Family Rights', I called for reform of the rules governing what is known as the parental power to create equality between parents with regard to their children.[1] The call was made at a time when the rights of parents of legitimate children had just been made equal by the Guardianship Act of 1993,[2] when the judgment of J van Zyl in *Van Erk v Holmer*[3] was being subjected to intense scrutiny and (largely negative) comment by judges and academic writers,[4] when the S A Law Commission was undertaking its project on the rights of unmarried fathers,[5] and when the Appellate Division, as it was still known, had been seized of but had not given judgment on the emotionally charged issue of the right of a natural father to access to his illegitimate child in *B v S*.[6] I repeated the exercise in 1996, in *The Law of Marriage*,[7] and was by then able to include

---

* Advocate of the High Court of South Africa, Professor and Executive Director, University of Pretoria.
1 See the chapter entitled 'Family Rights' in D van Wyk, J Dugard, B de Villiers & D Davis (eds) *Rights and Constitutionalism: The New South African Legal Order* Cape Town, Juta 1994 502 at 537-40.
2 192 of 1993.
3 1992 (2) SA 636 (W).
4 See *S* 1993 (2) SA 200 (W) and the unreported decisions referred to in the judgment, and the decision of the court *a quo* in *B v S* 1993 (2) SA 211 (W), which was later confirmed by the Appellate Division in *B v S* 1995 (3) SA 571 (A). The views of academic writers on the judgment are set out in June Sinclair (assisted by Jacqueline Heaton) *The Law of Marriage* Volume 1 Cape Town, Juta 1996 115 n 307.
5 See the Law Commission's *Investigation into the Legal Position of Illegitimate Children*, Project 38 of 1985 and its *Report on the Rights of a Father in respect of his Illegitimate Child*, Project 79 of 1994, which superseded Working Paper 44, Project 79 of 1993.
6 See *B v S* 1993 (2) SA 211 (W). The judgment of the Appellate Division was handed down in May 1995, and the case was reported in 1995 (3) SA 571 (A).
7 At 111-26.

comment on the draft legislation proposed by the Law Commission,[8] and on the finding of the Appellate Division in *B v S*[9] that a father of an illegitimate has no automatic right of access and that this state of affairs is not unfairly discriminatory. (The highest court stated that if there were sound sociological and policy reasons for affording fathers automatic rights in respect of their illegitimate children, then that was a matter for the legislature.)

My appraisal of the Law Commission's proposed legislation was not favourable. And my analysis of the judgment of JA Howie in *B v S* was not uncritical.[10] I expressed the view that the law governing extramarital children and the maternal preference rule in the award of custody on divorce were vulnerable to constitutional challenge[11] and I advocated a comprehensive recrafting of the rules governing children and parents, much broader than the intervention then envisaged by the Law Commission, which amounted to not much more than statutory articulation of the common law governing extramarital children. Joint custody[12] as the presumptive starting point on divorce was recommended, unless the circumstances warranted a departure from that general principle. The recommendations for legislative equality between parents were and remain controversial, and thus deserve justificatory explication. My motives were to see codified, in order to simplify, the complex mix of

---

8   See the 1994 Report referred to in n 5 above.
9   See n 6 above.
10 See Sinclair *The Law of Marriage* at 117-20.
11 The *Law of Marriage* 122 and also at 154-8. I Schafer 'Joint Custody' (1987) 104 *SALJ* 149 at 154-5 and B Clark and B van Heerden 'Joint Custody: Perspectives and Permutations'(1995) 112 *SALJ* 315 at 318 share this view.
12 The meaning of a joint custody award needs clarification. It need not and should not entail the child's moving from one parent to the other on a weekly or monthly basis. See I Scafer op cit 155-8, who discusses the two components of joint custody, ie physical custody and legal custody, and explains that joint custody should imply shared legal custody, permitting both parents to participate in decisions about the child's future, while it resides with one parent, the other having rights of access. For further information on the varying configurations of joint custody orders in other jurisdictions, see the academic writing cited in Sinclair *The Law of Marriage* 153-8. The Law Commission's Issue Paper 13, Project 110 on *The Review of the Child Care Act*, dated 18 April 1998, contains important explanations of the international trend away from traditional custody and access awards towards 'contact' and 'residence' orders on divorce: par 6.4.2.

common law and statutory rules governing children, and to see equality between women and men promoted, without compromising the welfare of children. They are unchanged, and it is heartening to see substantial movement in that direction, particularly in the most recent work of the Law Commission,[13] to which I shall refer below.

Quite apart from the suggestions pertaining to these specific issues, however, was the more general suggestion for a better way of thinking about parental power, as parental responsibility. By the time the two pieces mentioned above appeared, the comparative literature was replete with articles on the shift away from parental power towards parental responsibility. Indeed, JA Howie in *B v S* had already articulated the fact that in these matters we are dealing with the extramarital 'child's right to have access or to be spared access'.[14] The rather obvious point was therefore made that the rights of the child as enshrined in the Constitution now dominated the debate, not the rights of parents. Disappointment was expressed about the fact that the academic writing at that time was overwhelmingly devoted to attempting to resolve the *Van Erk* versus *B v S* impasse, by way of extensive comment on the narrow private law focus of the output of the Law Commission on unmarried fathers.[15] I drew attention to the fact that that writing seemed to be missing something, namely the constitutional dimension of the debate. Questions alluded to but not squarely confronted asked about the broader implications of the contest between parents to be treated equally with regard to rearing their children, and about the rights of children as postulated in the Constitution and in the United Nations Convention on the Rights of the Child, to which South Africa became a signatory on 16 June 1995.

It was clear that at that time we were working within the narrow confines of the old paradigm, desperately trying to find the meaning of the expression 'best interests of the child', but

---

13 Issue Paper 13, Project 110 on *The Review of the Child Care Act*, dated 18 April 1998.
14 1995 (3) SA 571 (A) 581-2.
15 Sinclair *The Law of Marriage* 120-3. See the criticism of the persistent adherence to parental-rights discourse by B Clark and B van Heerden 1995 *SALJ* 315.

failing to locate the debate outside conventional private law thinking. To the extent that we were confronting issues of gender equality, we confined even that debate to a contest between the mother and the father of a child born out of wedlock, leaving out the different treatment of fathers of legitimate and fathers of children born out of wedlock, and often ignoring or neglecting the child's own rights to know and bond with both its parents.[16]

No wonder then that the legislative intervention that ensued from this impoverished debate, the Natural Fathers of Children Born out of Wedlock Act of 1997, was a non-event that has been recognised already to have been inadequate.[17] Note its name. The legislation is about fathers, special types of fathers. It is apparently not, first and foremost, about parents, or about children. It should have been called something like 'The Parental Responsibility for and Rights of Extramarital Children Act'. The truth is that the act does not tamper with the preferential status accorded to mothers of children born out of wedlock. It does little more than restate the broad principle and concomitant implications of the common law that 'een moeder

---

16 A distinctly 'protectionist' attitude to women is evident in some of the writing, and more especially in the reasoning of the Law Commission in its 1994 justification for denying equal rights to fathers. See further Sinclair *The Law of Marriage* 121, esp nn 321 and 323.

17 86 of 1997. It enacts powers for the court to award access, custody or guardianship to the father of a child born out of wedlock, powers the court in any event had at common law. The legislation also sets out a list of circumstances which the court must take into consideration in exercising its powers. Many of these, and in particular the best interests of the child, are obvious and would have featured anyway, in any court's consideration of such an issue. The act also purported to rectify the complaint of discrimination made in *Fraser v Children's Court, Pretoria North* 1997 (2) SA 261 (CC). That case concerned the rule flowing from the common law but embodied in a statute (s 18(4) of the Child Care Act 74 of 1983). The rule dispenses with the need for the father's involvement in and consent to the adoption of his child born out of wedlock. The legislative provision was declared unfairly discriminatory, and the judge referred the matter to the legislature so that it could perform its rightful function of rectifying the matter. But the 1997 legislation provides only that the father must be given notice of the impending adoption. The Adoption Matters Amendment Bill 80 of 1998 goes further. It repeals the attempt in s 6 of the 1997 Act to deal with the problem of consent to adoption and requires the consent of the father to the child's adoption, but only provided he has acknowledged himself to be the father. The Bill sets out circumstances in which the consent of the father can be dispensed with. The fundamental inequality between the parents, however, central to this discussion, remains intact, and the question is whether it is justified.

maakt geen bastaard', the subtext of which implies that we still accept the outmoded notion of the Roman-Dutch era that the father of such a child is, by and large, an uncaring vagabond who 'got the poor woman pregnant and wouldn't marry her'.

The persisting assumption, a hangover from a bygone era and very different social mores, is that a lack of contact between a father and his child is invariably potestative to the father. The assumption fails to recognise the child's own preference, which may or may not be influenced by the mother's preference. And it fails to recognise that the reason for a father's failure to know, support and bond with his child may be the result of the mother's own decisions in this regard. In what ways might the preservation of this assumption be inimical to the project of equality to which women have committed so much? As long as women go on striving for equal opportunity in the workplace by calling for a restructuring of that place to take due account of the human lifecycle; as long as we continue to proclaim that the ideal worker is not necessarily a man with no child care responsibilities; as long as we insist that the burden of child rearing must be shared by men so that we can attain our full potential and cease to suffer the human capital depreciation flowing from motherhood that fills the pages of feminist journals; as long as we do these things, and we must do them, we are going to struggle to justify the simultaneous claim for special treatment as a starting point in the law governing parental responsiblity. We are not going to be able to say that in all matters equality is fine and we want it now, but in relation to children born out of wedlock, regardless of the fact that many are born in stable, marriage-like relationships, we want the advantage. We want the law to say that we are presumptively better parents than our children's fathers are, and that if they can prove the opposite then fine, they can visit their children or have custody or even share guardianship. We are also not going to be able to assume that on divorce the law should prefer us because we are primary caretakers, while at the same time claiming that we ought not to be primary caretakers – our husbands and partners should share parental responsibility equally. In any event, most of us have to go out to work on divorce, if we were not working before. The old assumption that a divorced woman would be supported until death or remarriage and would stay at home and rear the children is dead. So, maybe the father, with his more senior position,[18] and consequent greater flexibility regarding work time, might be in a better position to be a primary caretaker after divorce than a mother. We need to confront these realities rather than shelter behind the protectionism of the law.

There is a more subtle argument here, and maybe a more insidiously harmful effect of legal protectionism that must be stated: special treatment traps women within the locus of their current inferiority. It publicly declares that women cannot compete and because of their inability to compete they need to be regarded differently. It cultivates a mindset of inferiority. We need to tell ourselves that we are not merely victims of discrimination, but we are survivors. And we will demand our due wherever we are treated unfairly. What we are seeking is a changed societal attitude towards working mothers and the willingness of working fathers to share the parenting responsibility. Employers must understand that men have homemaking duties. Men must understand that their lives too have been impoverished by the stereotyped role allocations that dominate our history. The system cannot have the benefit of the expectation that we will be financially self-sufficient, and make a contribution to the cost of the upkeep of the home, and continue alone to do the double shift of working outside the home and 'keeping' it when the day's work in the office is done. While we go on making the simultaneous claims of equality and special treatment, we damage our own enterprise. And we bring up our children in the same mindset, ensuring for them the same inequality that we have experienced.

This view is likely to be interpreted by some as anti-feminist. But the changes I have suggested are finding very broad acceptance in jurisdictions with which we routinely compare ourselves. And they are gaining acceptance here. No one would

---

18 Women, in the main, occupy more junior and less well paid positions.

deny that single mothers experience hardship and difficulties occasioned by interfering, uncaring fathers of their children. Many such fathers do not comply with their obligations to maintain their offspring and it would seem unfair to accord them the same legal rights as mothers. My view is that the law should not proceed from the assumption that such dereliction is the norm. It should assume that in most cases both parents love their children. Pathological situations should be dealt with as exceptions. Maintenance obligations should be properly and cheaply enforced, and mothers should be ensured easy and inexpensive access to the courts to alter equal parental rights whenever it is appropriate to do so.[19]

Attention should now be given to some examples of the striking movement that has taken place in the past few years within the terrain of the content of the law governing the relationships of parents and children.

The purpose is to locate us within the context of parental reponsibility, and to produce a fresh mindset when we re-evaluate the rules we have chosen for children born out wedlock and the practice we endorse regarding custody on divorce. I shall then conclude with some remarks about the danger of over legislating, and the limits of what the law can achieve to alleviate the plight of our children.

In 1996 Raylene Keightley edited a book entitled *Children's Rights*.[20] In it are thirteen essays on children covering a wide range of topics. The book manifests an entirely new approach

---

19 See Sinclair *The Law of Marriage* 124-6. During discussion at the Conference on 30 October 1998 in Pretoria, it emerged that the Law Commission is thinking of proposing a change in the law that would accord fathers of children born out of wedlock equal rights of guardianship with mothers in cases where parents who, for example, live together in a marriage-like relationship, register this fact and their agreement that parental power should be shared equally. The proposal has substantial merit. It would certainly alleviate the inequality experienced by such fathers, but only in cases where the mother of the child agrees. Making equal treatment of the parents by the law contingent upon agreement and hence potestative to the parent who already has full rights, namely the mother, does nothing to assist the father confronted by a woman who is (unreasonably) hostile. He is left to litigate for equal treatment, and the question of the fairness of such a situation will thus remain.
20 Published by Juta, Cape Town. Also published as 1996 *Acta Juridica*.

to the subject. In her comprehensive and insightful overview of the contributions, Keightley reminds us that chidren's issues are no longer confined to issues of private law.[21] Children are the bearers of constitutional rights and fathers are ever increasingly applying for custody, she notes, perhaps more aware of their own constitutional entitlements. The inevitable clash of rights looms large here.[22]

In her contribution to the book, Julia Sloth-Nielsen[23] cites the views of two prominent politicians that are revealing: Tony Leon, during the debate on whether to put children's rights into the final Constitution,[24] said that to do so is like 'chicken soup' – it can do no harm.[25] His view was widely shared across the political spectrum. A question to which I return later is whether we are doing no more than sipping chicken soup as we grapple with children's rights. Sloth Nielsen also quotes, within the context of a discussion on *Kruger v Minister of Correctional Services*,[26] former president Mandela, justifying his decision to single out imprisoned mothers for amnesty: '... I was motivated predominantly by a concern for chidren who had been deprived of the nurturing and care which their mothers would ordinarily have provided.'[27] Consider for a moment the cases we read about involving sexual abuse of children by their mothers' partners, with the collusion of their mothers (who, I concede, may be afraid of their partners) and decide whether it is axiomatic and inexorable that depriving a child of his or her mother's care is worse than depriving a child of his or her father's care. I do not think we can go on saying these things and at the same time claim that we are striving for an egalitarian dispensation in family law. Mandela's words are evocative of an era when we adhered to the notion that parenting is women's work. We have rejected this view of the world.

---

21 At 1.
22 At 2.
23 Entitled 'Chicken Soup or Chainsaws: Some Implications of the Constitutionalisation of Children's Rights in South Africa' op cit n 20 above, at 6.
24 Act 108 of 1996.
25 See Sloth-Nielsen at 9.
26 1995 (2) SA 803 (T).
27 Sloth-Nielsen at 23.

Ann Palmer's essay[28] contains what she terms 'an alarming view' from the 1985 case of *Willers v Serfontein*:[29]

> 'To preserve a living bond of love and respect with an absent father, a weekend per month and alternate school holidays will suffice, if such contact is used constructively and wisely'.[30]

This language is unfortunate, to say the least. Palmer contrasts this unacceptable (older) view,[31] with that taken on joint custody in the 1993 case of *Venton*,[32] where the judge, justifying a joint custody preference, commented that if after a joint custody order is made a dispute arises, 'that will hardly be a calamity. The court will simply have to be approached to resolve the dispute.'[33] Spot on. And this view is reinforced by the 1996 judgment in *Van der Linde v Van der Linde*,[34] where the judge said that the function of 'mothering is also part of a man's being'.[35] He questioned whether the quality of a parental role can be determined by gender, and he attacked the gender stereotyping to which we have become accustomed. *V v V*[36] is the latest case (October 1998) to proclaim the new, albeit contested, era. The court had to deal with a father seeking custody and a mother seeking joint custody, where the mother was involved in a lesbian relationship which the father believed was inimical to the interests of the children. Unlike the court in *van Rooyen*,[37] which

---

28 Entitled 'The Best Interests Criterion: An Overview of its Application in Custody Decisions Relating to Divorce in the Period 1985-1995' Keightley op cit 98 at 107.
29 1985 (2) SA 591 (T).
30 At 595.
31 And that taken in *Schlebusch* 1988 (4) SA 518 (E), where joint custody was refused in the face of a consent paper asking for it.
32 1993 (3) SA 72 (SECLD).
33 At 766. This case accords with the earlier decision in *Kastan v Kastan* 1985 (3) SA 235 (C).
34 1996 (3) SA 509 (O).
35 At 515. Some might be tempted to criticise the gendered language of 'mothering' and argue that, if the judge had really escaped the stereotyping he challenges, he would have chosen the word 'parenting'. There is force in this argument. But let us not diminish the big step forward in his thinking. It is refreshing, to say the least. The point about shared parenting is arguably more forcefully made by asserting that men can mother.
36 1998 (4) SA 169 (C).
37 1994 (2) SA 325 (W).

held that lesbianism sends 'the wrong signal',[38] it held that the Constitution proscribes a finding that homosexual orientation is abnormal. It would be wrong to curtail a mother's access because of her lifestyle, it said. Joint custody was ordered.

These decisions evidence a massive shift in the mindset of the white male judiciary. They are refreshing. Belinda van Heerden and Julia Sloth-Nielsen describe what is happening as 'an impending revolution in child and family law'.[39] Of great overall significance is the statement in *V v V*[40] that

'There is no doubt that over the last number of years the emphasis in thinking in regard to questions of relationships between parents and their children has shifted from a concept of parental power of the parents to one of parental responsiblity and children's rights.'[41]

Belinda van Heerden is heading a project of the South Africa Law Commission entitled 'Review of the Child Care Act'.[42] The literature list attached to the 1998 Issue Paper is not merely impressive;[43] it is as daunting as the thorough and meticulous coverage of every imaginable question regarding chidren's legislation. The questions are all there. The answers remain elusive. But for the first time we are seeing a commendable, holistic approach towards developing a children's code and proper attention to comparative developments. The Issue Paper sets out the demands of the UN Convention on the Rights of the Child and of our own Constitution, so that we are not misled about the boundaries within which we are working. In relation to the topics under discussion, we are reminded that article 9 of the UN Convention enunciates the right of a child not to be separated from its **parent** (mother or father); that article 18 recognises common parental responsibilities; and that these princi-

---

38 At 329-30. See also *Pinion* 1994 (2) SA 725 (D).
39 In 'Putting Humpty Dumpty Back Together Again: Towards Restructuring Families' and Chidren's Lives in South Africa' (1998) 115 *SALJ* 156.
40 1998 (4) SA 169 (C).
41 At 176.
42 See n 13 above.
43 Pages xiv-xxi of the Issue Paper.

ples accord with the demand of our Constitution that children be accorded the right to parental (not maternal) care.[44] The provisions do not differentiate between legitimate children and children born out wedlock.

The rapid shift away from parental rights and towards parental responsibility in the legislation of the nineties that has occurred in Scotland,[45] England [46] and Australia[47] as well as the laws of several African states are pertinently described by the commission.[48] In Australia, equal status with mothers is accorded automatically to the fathers of children born out of wedlock, and we are told, encouragingly, that, in the light of local and comparative developments, the commission is looking again at the question of extramarital children.[49]

K F Kaltenborn and R Lempp, writing in 1998, set out copiously the current position in Germany.[50] In their piece these authors stress the wishes of the child; the child's right to access to both its parents; the fact that joint custody is the norm in Germany after divorce and that circumstances justifying deviation from this norm are set out statutorily; and the rejection of the primary caretaker criterion to determine custody disputes.[51] Most importantly, they state that very few custody cases reach the courts because the law affects the way in which parents settle their disputes privately.[52] It seems clear that the German law pushes parents in the direction of joint responsibility. It does

---

44 In section 28(1)(*b*) of Act 108 of 1996.
45 See the Children Scotland Act 1995 par 10.3.2.
46 See the Children Act 1989 but, more importantly, the Family Law Act 1996, which requires parents to honour their responsilbities to their children before they may remarry: John Dewar 'The Normal Chaos of Family Law' (1998) 61 *Modern LR* 467 at 476.
47 See the Family Law Reform Act 1995.
48 See par 10 of the Issue Paper.
49 Par 11.1 of the Issue Paper.
50 'The Welfare of the Child in Custody Disputes after Parental Separation or Divorce' (1998) 12 *Int J of Law, Policy and the Fam* 74.
51 The authors criticise the fact that the primary caretaker criterion emphasises quantity of time spent with the child rather than quality and relies on evidence of what the parent does rather than how the child responds. They declare a shift to the advantage of fathers, based on their good relationships with their children, and state that their data match those of Mnookin for the state of California, op cit 101.
52 Op cit 102.

not seek to pit them against each other in an adversarial contest over their respective 'rights' over their children.

A fascinating study of parental attitudes in Australia to shared responsibility is documented by Kathleen Funder.[53] This author stresses that the 'winners' and 'losers' mindset encouraged by the Family Law Act of 1975 has been eradicated in the 1995 legislation. The aspiration is to discourage ideas of ownership of children and to recognise fully that children need contact with both parents.[54] The Act provides that 'children have the right to know and be cared for by both their parents, regardless of whether their parents are married, separated, have never married, or have never lived together'.[55]

Although fully shared responsibility is more controversial in relation to a parent who has never lived with the child, public opinon reflects that this is the preferred starting premise of the law, to be departed from only where the interests of the child call for it.[56] A national survey on parental responsibility was conducted in Australia in 1994. In response to a question, 'Do you think that children should be in contact with both their parents on a regular basis when parents are, respectively, married, separated/divorced, never married, have never lived together?', the preponderance of opinion, in all cases was 'yes'. In relation to parents 'never married' (which captures cohabitees), the response to the question was 65% 'always', 25% 'mostly', and less than 10% 'sometimes'. No response of 'rarely' or 'never' was received. In relation to parents who had never lived together, the response to the question was (roughly)[57] 42% 'always', 24% 'mostly', 28% 'sometimes', 4% 'rarely' and 2% 'never'. These results reflect a startling tolerance for diverse lifestyles. They may even (taken together with other data) suggest that public opinion is 'in advance' of the 1995 Act, rendering it,

---

53 'The Australian Family Law Reform Act (1995) and Public Attitudes to Parental Responsibility' (1998) 12 *Int J of Law, Policy and the Fam* 47.
54 At 49.
55 S 60B(2) of the Act, quoted by Funder op cit 50.
56 Op cit 51.
57 The figure (Fig 3) appearing at 56 does not specify the percentages, but these are detectable, at least roughly, from the graphic.

in the words of the author 'a milestone on a road already travelled'.⁵⁸ Funder concludes that 'Australians hold to a set of core parental responsibilities, regardless of their own family and marital histories or conditions. This fairly robust homogeneity is a comfortable starting point for family law ...'.⁵⁹

Let me recall at this point that the argument being advanced in this paper is that the law should assume non-pathology. It should cater for the common case. It should assume that both parents ordinarily love their children. It should provide a basis from which parents will negotiate on an equal footing, within the legal framework, the outcome of breakdown of their intimate relationships, or the fact that their child is the product of a relationship that has not entailed living together.

Our law regarding children born out of wedlock and custody on divorce assumes that mothers need special favours; that unless the law treats them differently, fathers will procure privileges they do not deserve and children will as a consequence suffer some unarticulated hardship. Our law radiates the message that mothers are better parents than fathers and that fathers have a general proclivity of defaulting on their responsibilities to their children. If that is the sorry state of our society, we should be alert to changing it via appropriate education and counselling and efficient, expeditious and inexpensive enforcement of parental obligations.⁶⁰ One way to assist a change in attitude is to make the promise of equality expressed in our Constitution a reality and proceed from there to invoke the court's powers to alter the norm whenever the circumstances require it. To insist on a starting point that excludes fathers from the ambit of shared parenting will harden their attitudes and foster

---

58 Op cit 48.
59 Op cit 60.
60 The maintenance defaulter comes to mind here. The remedy for this default is enforcement coupled with welfare where this is needed, an issue beyond the scope of this paper, but vital, and receiving the attention of the Law Commission in the project on maintenance, headed by Sandra Burman. The remedy should not be to deprive all unmarried fathers (even those who live with the mothers of their children in marriage-like relationships) of the opportunity to nurture a positive relationship with their children unless and until they can prove to a court that they are 'normal' fathers.

undesirable conduct. It will, I suspect, ultimately be detrimental to the cause of the very women who assert that the law should favour them. To insist on such a starting point is also a violation of the child's right to grow up loving and respecting both parents until one or both demonstrates that he or she is not worthy of that love and respect. The law has no business making assumptions based on outdated role allocations that are inimical to the rights of parents and children alike.

I wish to conclude with some remarks about the reach of the law. What can the law achieve? Is there any downside associated with legislating?

What we have to recognise here is that there is a tension between the discourse of rights, which is rule based, and the discourse of best interests, which is based on the exercise of discretion. We say, almost glibly, that children and parents have rights, legal rights, enshrined constitutional rights. At the same time, we assert that all these rights are subject to the best interests of the child, which are consitutionally paramount. John Dewar has recently written an excellent piece in the *Modern Law Review* entitled 'The Normal Chaos of Family Law'.[61] He contrasts the rights model, based on rules, with the utility model, based on the child's interests. Out of these competing models he perceives a 'normative anarchy'. We go through phases of leaning more heavily on discretion (as can be seen from the eighties movement regarding division of property on divorce) and then we revert to rules, (as is evident in the current articulation of children's rights).

But he is not upset by the ensuing chaos. Rather, he says, the constant tension is constructive, and leads to a situation where modern legalism is operating through 'indirect symbolic controls', radiating messages to assist private ordering rather than confering measurable entitlements on parents and their children.[62]

Dewar's article made me look again at the Law Commis-

---

61 Op cit n 46 above.
62 At 474.

sion's Issue Paper[63] and the collection of essays in Raylene Keightley's book[64] to remind myself of the complex array of initiatives that have been undertaken in the realm of children's welfare generally in South Africa over the past few years. We learn of the spontaneous abandonment of corporal punishment,[65] the moves against the incarceration of children,[66] inter-ministerial, inter-disicplinary working groups[67] trying to find a holistic way to deal coherently with children at risk, and a host of other initiatives which I commend to you again.

But the materials also remind us of a deep societal malaise. The Law Commission's paper states that child abandonment is rife in South Africa,[68] that the SAPS Child Protection Unit dealt with 35 000 cases of child abuse in 1997[69] and that poverty is the root cause of neglect and abuse.

It encourages work being done on a national welfare strategy. It contains the especially chilling observation that there may be a danger that government spending might decline as we pass more laws.[70] It wisely warns that legislation is not the end goal.[71] Legislation is no more than the end of the beginning of the war against harm to children.

Where are we then? Are we doing the right things? I think so. I am enormously impressed by the range and scope of the Law Commission's current work in this field. When I studied the Issue Paper I felt reassured, almost comfortable. It seemed to me that we are radiating the right messages.

Then I started to write this paper and reflect more deeply on the challenges. And I saw an article in the press, the horror of which I shall refer to in a moment. And I fell again into a state of anxiety on realising how easily I had succumbed to com-

---

63 Supra n 13.
64 Supra n 20.
65 See Julia Sloth-Nielsen's in *Children's Rights* at 14-17.
66 Sloth-Nielsen in *Children's Rights* 18-22.
67 See par 6.4 of the Law Commission's Issue Paper (op cit n 13 above).
68 Par 4.2.8 of the Issue Paper.
69 Par 4.2.8.
70 Par 11.2.
71 Par 11.4.

placency. Raylene Keightley,[72] I recalled, had uttered a sobering reminder of the limitations of the law. She had warned against the complacency that can flow from adoption of international conventions and the enactment of bright and shiny new laws.[73] I was prompted to read Michael King's piece in Keightley's book, 'Against Chidren's Rights'.[74] I started to wonder whether we are merely sipping Tony Leon's chicken soup. Are we in danger of saying and believing that we are doing all the right things? 'All is well on the children front. Children have rights that are protected by law.'

It would be hard to deny that our lives are filled with the wonderment of our new Constitution. We adduce it in defence of anything we do not like about our society, and as testimony to the achievement of everything of which we want to be proud. The advent of our new Constitution delivered to us, like manna from heaven, that magical thing called 'democracy'. We are building 'a rights culture', so that we can all insist on our rights.

The question that keeps nagging is: 'What kind of society are we (lawyers) helping to create?' Have we become smug at our success? Is there any reason to be fearful of the rights culture, the emphasis we are placing on individual liberty and individual happiness?

I have written at some length on this topic,[75] drawing on the riveting work of Mary Ann Glendon.[76] Glendon's warning is that the intemperate rhetoric of rights, encouraged by the legal prefession, has bred Americans who live and think as atomised individuals, all rights and a diminished sense of reponsibility. Glendon singles out constitutional law, criminal law and family law as crucial terrains within which lawyers can define the kind of society being brought into being.

---

72 Op cit n 20 above, at 3.
73 Op cit at 5.
74 Keightley *Children's Rights* at 28.
75 'Ways of Seeing – "Lawyering" for a new Society in South Africa' in J Eekelaar and T Nhlapo *The Changing Family* Oxford, Hart Publishing 1998 at 493.
76 *Rights Talk – The Impoverishment of Legal Discourse* New York, Free Press 1991 and *A Nation under Lawyers* New York, Farrar, Strauss Giroux 1994.

The Canadian author, Margaret Hall, writing about a Ministry for Children in British Columbia,[77] concludes that debates about child abuse are really about the nature of the good society. So what kind of society is one where Sonja Michalski runs the South African branch of an American organisation called 'Children of the Underground'?[78]

This organisation assists abused women and children to flee the country and slip past immigration authorities so that they can create new identities abroad. The story appeared in an article supplementing a headline offer of a reward of R11 million for information leading to the discovery of the whereabouts of one Ellen Dever Shah and her two daughters. Her husband, said to have abused her and the children while they lived in the United States, is an extremely wealthy American who wanted his children back. Their mother was concealing them from him, here in South Africa. Interpol Director, David Bruce, remarked that it was disturbing that bounty hunters were out looking for the woman and her children. Mrs Shah is reported to be one of more than 200 American women currently underground with their children. Michalski reports South African cases so desperate that she had to get the women and children out of the country 'to avoid tragedy'. She has sent several to Canada and Britain. They are kept in safe houses or shelters until they can construct new identities and new lives in foreign countries.

Need I say more about the limitations of law and of lawyers?

---

77 'A Ministry for Children: Abandoning the Interventionist Debate in British Columbia' (1998) 12 *Int J of Law, Policy and the Fam* 121 at 143.
78 See the *Saturday Star* 17 October 1998.

Child labour

Ms Tshidi Mayimele-Hashatse*

1 INTRODUCTION

Most people would ask the question whether child labour is a problem in South Africa. Yes, it is a problem. The government through the Department of Labour, estimates that there are 500 000 child labourers in the country. The Network Against Child Labour in its annual report in 1996 estimated that there were approximately 200 000 children between the ages of 10 and 14 and another 200 000 between 15 and 18 who were working then as child labourers. It is difficult to know what the true figures are and the more there is growth in poverty and drug abuse, the more one would imagine the child labour figures soar. Those children most likely to be exploited and used as child labourers fall into the following categories:
- **Rural or farm children:** These children often do not go beyond elementary schooling and even when they are in school they work after school hours, especially in harvest time and other labour intensive times on the farms.
- **Street children:** These children work to support themselves and some researchers say that some children who do not particularly come from unbearable home environments are lured to the streets by the promise of earning money. The abuse of alcohol and drugs also leads

---

* Practising Attorney, Sandton. As the former deputy director of the Centre for Human Rights at the University of Pretoria, Tshidi Mayimele-Hashatse headed the Child Labour Project *Exploring some dimensions of Child Labour in South Africa* C Molope, S Thabalala and W Schurink W (eds).

to the need for these children to do any kind of paying work to support their habits.
- **Orphaned children and Aids victims:** Children who are orphaned and fall through the cracks of the family and welfare system can end up being child labourers. The spread of Aids is increasing and the number of orphans is also rising. Where these children are orphaned by Aids, their families and communities may even shun them.
- **Girl child:** Statistics still suggest that girl children are less likely to complete high school education especially on the farms. These children often leave school after primary schooling.
- **Drugs and gangs:** Children involved in these activities often have to earn money to support their activities and addictions. Very often they are employed in the drug trade.
- **Disability:** Research shows that disabled children are less likely to be educated fully and often drop out even when their capabilities could allow for further education. An interesting angle to this problem is that they often end up in upliftment and income-producing programmes where the disabled produce crafts and other goods. These programmes, particularly those initiated and run by disabled communities do not seem averse to accepting school going children.

2 SECTORS

The sectors that have been identified as those most likely to use child labour are agriculture, brick-yards and coal-yards, the taxi industry (as queue marshals, washers), street hawking, domestic labour, sex trade, newspaper vending, entertainment (e.g. music, television, theatre, etc.), sweat shops (especially in Cape Town) and family businesses.

The employment of children in one sector as opposed to another is viewed differently by society and the condemnation of some industries is also less than for others. For instance, children in television, even when this interferes with their schooling, other activities and development, is largely approved of by society. Children on farms, for instance, are put to work at times by their parents rather than by the farmer. The farmer in some instances does not even see the children as his employees. The children help their parents who get paid by how much fruit they have picked and so on. So the more the members of the family are involved in the activity, the more the income for the family.

3 CAUSES

Some of the causes of child labour that have been identified through research are poverty; breakdown of families and especially of African family values; traditional prejudices and excuses about the role of the child; and the incapacity of the education system to deal with all the children and their different needs which leads to alienation of certain kinds of children.

Furthermore, children are cheap labour. Children are more docile workers. Children from minorities are the ones most often used (ethnic, religous and foreign minorities especially with an illegal immigrant status).

Issues such as society's reaction to child labour often set the climate of acceptance or indifference, which allows child labour to exist. Lack of proper government policy or failure in administering a good policy also contributes to the existence and growth of child labour.

Child labour seems to be preferred in some industries even when there is high unemployment and an abundance of adults who would work for less than minimum wages. It seems that employers would rather risk prosecution for using child labour than exploit adults and risk prosecution and union activity. Perhaps child labour continues to exist because, even though there is the threat of prosecution, there is a lack of sufficient and regular surveillance that can lead to prosecution. The intervention and enforcement mechanisms do not seem to be enough to induce change. There does not seem to be any fear of punishment.

4 LEGAL FRAMEWORK

There are a number of documents that form the legal framework for South Africa. Some of the most important ones are referred to below.

4.1 Constitution of the Republic of South Africa[1]
Section 28 of the Constitution deals with children's rights and in particular subsection 1 (e) and (f) deal with child labour. This section says that each child has the right
'to be protected from exploitative labour practices'
and
'not to be required or permitted to work or provide services that –
  (i) are inappropriate for a person of that child's age
  (ii) place at risk the child's well-being, education, physical or mental health or spiritual, moral or social development;'

4.2 Other legislation
At the domestic level additional legislation that is relevant includes the Basic Conditions of Employment Act,[2] which at section 43 sets the minimum ages for employment as 15 and makes it illegal to employ someone below school-leaving age. Children between these ages may not be employed in environments that could be hazardous to their health, well-being and development. This Act effectively outlaws forced labour. The South African Schools Act[3] is also important to the extent that it makes

---
1   108 of 1996.
2   75 of 1997.
3   84 of 1996.

it mandatory for children to be sent to school until they are 15 years of age or have completed the ninth grade.

4.3 International and regional instruments

The United Nations Convention on the Rights of the Child is the foremost international instrument to be referred to when dealing with children's rights despite any objections that have been levelled at this document. In particular articles 31, 32, 33, 34 and 36 must be taken into consideration in a debate on child labour (see United Nations International Convention on the Rights of the Child, page 145 to 146).

The similarities between section 28 of the South African Constitution and article 32 are notable. The duties placed upon South Africa by the above articles of the Convention are clear from the reading of the Convention. The writer's opinion is that South Africa has legislative and policy frameworks, but is lacking in the administrative, social and educational, as well implementation obligations.

The African Charter on the Welfare and the Rights of the Child[4] says that children must be protected from all forms of economic exploitation and from engaging in any work that is likely to interfere with their physical, mental, spiritual, moral or social development. The substance of this Charter is similar to the other instruments and legislation referred to earlier. It therefore seems that there is general agreement on how and what to protect children from in the area of child labour.

The International Labour Organisation Convention sets the internationally agreed minimum age at 15. Children between 13 and 15 can be allowed to do light work that does not harm their health or development.

---

4 Art 15.

5　INTERNATIONAL PERSPECTIVE

Unicef in 1998 published statistics that show that there are still large numbers of children of school-going age not in school in many parts of the world. The percentages are as follows:

	Boys	Girls
Sub-Saharan Africa	39	45
Middle East and North Africa	15	24
East Africa and the Pacific	2	4
South Asia	25	37
Latin America	11	10

Over 90% of children in developing countries go to school, 75 % complete the first four years. One hundred and thirty million children are not in school and 60% of these are girls. These Unicef statistics indicate the existence of a serious and pervasive problem. It is also very clear that it is the developing nations that do not seem to be able to keep their children in school. These children end up as child labourers. What is not clear is whether they leave school to go and work or work because they are not in school. Poverty and other living conditions make these kinds of questions difficult to answer.

The International Labour Organisation (ILO) estimates that there are 250 million children worldwide who are labourers and that 50 % of them are in full-time employment. A hundred and fifty to two hundred million children do unpaid domestic labour in the family where they are almost exclusively responsible for the household and siblings while the parents work long hours and double shifts. According to the ILO 60% of these children are found in Asia, 32% in Africa, 7% in Latin America, and the numbers are growing in Central and Eastern Europe.

The ILO and Unicef have been involved in programmes to eliminate child labour in many parts of the world. Some of their strategies will be discussed here. Most of the programmes are aimed at removing children below the age of fourteen from the labour force. The programmes involve the ILO or Unicef, manufacturers and sometimes governments or their agencies. These stakeholders often begin by entering into a memorandum of understanding. These kinds of agreements have been entered into in places like Bangladesh and India.

Once an agreement is reached to keep children out of formal employment, different kinds of programmes are instituted with employers who provide incentives and monitoring. Examples of these programmes include the following :

5.1 Labelling method

This is when goods carry information on the label that informs consumers that no child labour was used in the manufacturing process. This method has been criticised for not always backing up the claims on the label with independent monitoring. Human rights NGOs especially feel they should have the right to do random inspections. Questions have been raised about the certainty that subcontractors have also followed the standards. Again here monitoring by the manufacturer or independent sources is called for.

In 1995 in India the Kalleen labelling system was initiated which was administered by a quasi-government body. Carpet exporters were registered and issued with licenses for exporting. The Ministry of Commerce, using subscription fees from manufacturers, funded the project. Some of the money raised was used to rehabilitate former child labourers through the welfare system. Periodic monitoring is an essential ingredient to this system.

5.2 Certification method

There are different ways in which manufacturers can be certified for compliance with child labour agreements or legislation. The certification can be done by national governments, independent auditors or inspectors or international NGOs. Manufacturers can be certified for some or all of these factors: no child labour; safe working environment; respect for unionisation; implementation of minimum working hours; and payment of the minimum wage.

In addition to the certification process, factories can also enter into implementation timetables in order to comply fully with the agreements or the law. Progress is then documented and monitored. The certification programmes can be voluntary or compulsory.

India, Nepal and Pakistan have carpet industries that have been notorious for using child labourers. The children are used for activities such as spinning, unravelling yarn, weaving, knitting, cutting and washing. Since 1994 the Rugmark manufacturers of carpets in these countries have entered into voluntary certification for producing without using child labour. Independent, credible and professional monitors have been used. In 1997 63 600 carpets from 164 producers were labelled. In India 22 800 random inspections were made at 18 400 outlets. In Nepal 1 754 visits were made to some of the 1 868 outlets.

5.3 Consumer and retailer pressure

It is ironic that child labourers in the so-called 'third world' are also employed in the process of manufacturing toys for children in the 'first world'. In India and Pakistan children have been known to be used to manufacture soccer balls which are in turn sold to well-known international companies like Reebok.

Reebok has now put the following conditions to the manufacturers: no one below the age of 15 can be involved in the manufacturing process; there must be external monitoring of the factories; and there should be social responsibility programmes in the educational sphere undertaken in the geographic area of the factory. Another company that has insisted on its suppliers complying with certification programmes is toy store giant Toys R US.

It has to be noted that consumers and retailers have the power to force manufacturers to comply with basic conditions.

6 CONCLUSION

A strategy for South Africa will work only if it includes organisations and institutions such as the South African Police Service (Child Protection Unit), the Labour Department's inspectors, employers unions, labour unions, parents and teachers associations, consumer unions, the Welfare Department, the business sector, NGOs, the justice system; and the Education Department.

As stated above, South Africa already has a sound legal framework and the only problem is in the implementation. In addition to this the different government departments must accept responsibility to do what falls within their areas of responsibility. The strategy has to be holistic and properly coordinated.

Juvenile justice reform: children's rights and responsibilities versus crime control

Ann Skelton*

1 INTRODUCTION

In describing the unfinished journey of juvenile justice reform in South Africa this paper will identify and examine three major themes that have influenced the process of law reform; children's rights, restorative justice and political will.

The paper then poses the question as to whether these fundamental influences still hold weight, or whether they are giving way to the political imperative of crime control.

2 MAJOR POSITIVE INFLUENCES ON THE DEVELOPMENT OF JUVENILE JUSTICE REFORM

If juvenile justice reform is viewed against the broader transition of South African society a number of key issues can be identified as having a major influence on the process and direction of reform.

The first of these is the recognition of children's rights, within a framework of national and international human rights standards.

---

* Director: Child Rights Project, Lawyers for Human Rights, Pietermaritzburg.

3 CHILDREN'S RIGHTS WITHIN A FRAMEWORK OF NATIONAL AND INTERNATIONAL HUMAN RIGHTS STANDARDS

Those working for the reform of juvenile justice in South Africa have placed the issue firmly within the ambit of children rights.[1] The reason for this can best be understood by looking at the socio-political background from which the fledgling ideas of about the need for reform in juvenile justice grew.

During the 1970s and 1980s in South Africa it was common for large numbers of children to be arrested and held in custody on charges relating to political activity or to be held without trial.[2] At the time, political organisations and human rights lawyers rallied to the assistance of many of these children. Their efforts centred on children involved in political activism, but during this period there were equally large numbers of children awaiting trial on crimes which were non-political in nature, except in the broader sense that the circumstances in which the majority of the children lived could also be traced to socio-economic ills caused by apartheid. As the number of political detentions waned during the late 1980s, the country's police cells and prisons continued to be occupied by large numbers of children caught up in the criminal justice system. In 1987 an international conference on children's rights was held in Zimbabwe, and this activated the beginnings of what was to become a strong child rights movement in South Africa. The National Children's Rights Committee (NCRC), a non-governmental organisation, was established in 1991 and many groups working on children's issues affiliated to it. This all took place before South Africa's first democratic elections. Despite this, and de-

---

1 See generally J Sloth-Nielsen 'Ratification of the UN Convention of the Rights of the Child: Some implications for South Africa' 1995 *SAJHR* 419; A Skelton 'Developing a juvenile justice system for South Africa : International instruments and restorative justice' 1996 *Acta Juridica* 180; J Sloth-Nielsen 'Chicken soup or chainsaws: Some implications of the constitutionalisation of children's rights in South Africa' 1996 *Acta Juridica* 6.
2 T Thipanyane 'Legal and procedural reform in South Africa' in *Justice for Children: challenges for policy and practice in sub-Saharan Africa* 1998 31.

spite the fact that South Africa had not yet ratified the United Nations Convention on the Rights of the Child, the NCRC spearheaded the writing of a National Plan of Action for Children, which is normally written by governments as the first step towards their fulfilment of obligations under the United Nations Convention on the Rights of the Child.

Because of the struggle to achieve basic human rights for all in South Africa, the focus on the need for a fair and equitable juvenile justice system emerged somewhat later than in many comparable countries. The first intensive calls for such reforms came about in the early 1990s, and emanated from a group of non-governmental organisations[3] (NGOs). Members of these organisations went into the courts, police cells and prisons to provide assistance to juveniles awaiting trial. The stories of the children they met were highlighted by the media in a carefully orchestrated campaign. The public began to listen, and radio talk shows elicited sympathetic responses. It was in September 1992 that 13-year-old Neville Snyman was beaten to death by older teenage cell mates while awaiting trial on a charge of housebreaking. The NGOs active in the field[4] issued a joint report, entitled 'Justice for the children : No child should be caged', in which calls were made for a juvenile justice system to be created which would centre on the rights of children.

The government of the day was moved finally to show some commitment to doing something about children in prison, and they set up a working group under the Department of Welfare to consider alternatives to imprisonment for children. For the first time government department officials began to debate the issues with the non-government sector, and a thawing of relationships began.

At the end of 1993 an international seminar entitled 'Children in Trouble with the Law' was hosted by the Community Law Centre in Cape Town. Various ideas for a new juvenile justice system for South Africa were put forward. From this con-

---

3 The main three organisations involved at this time were Community Law Centre (Western Cape), NICRO and Lawyers for Human Rights.
4 Ibid.

ference a grouping[5] was formed to draft policy and legislative proposals. Although these proposals did not enjoy any official status, they did capture the discourse[6] in the field of juvenile justice in South Africa, and many debates thereafter revolved around the ideas set forth in the proposals.

The constitutionalisation of children's rights was an exciting new era which dawned with the new political dispensation. The drafting of a new Constitution by the Constitutional Assembly provided a vital opportunity to ensure that protection for children accused of crimes be incorporated in the highest law of the land. Child rights organisations made submissions to the Constitutional Assembly, using international instruments as their departure point.[7] The final wording of the children's rights clause of the South African Constitution testifies to the fact that these efforts bore fruit. Section 28(1)(g) states that every child has the right

> 'not to be detained except as a measure of last resort, in which case, in addition to the rights the child enjoys under sections 12 and 35, the child may be detained only for the shortest possible appropriate period of time, and has the right to be –
> (i) kept separately from detained persons over the age of 18 years; and
> (ii) treated in a manner, and kept in conditions, that take account of the child's age;'.

In 1994 the issue of the juvenile sentence of whipping was brought before the newly created South African Constitutional

---

5 The grouping called itself the juvenile justice drafting consultancy and included the Community Law Centre (UWC), Lawyers for Human Rights, NICRO, Institute of Criminology (UCT), Child Welfare and the Community Peace Foundation.
6 D Pinnock, A Skelton and R Shapiro 'New juvenile justice legislation for South Africa – giving children a chance' (1994) 3 *SACJ* 338.
7 The Legal Committee of National Children's Rights Committee, an umbrella body comprising a number of NGOs, put forward a strong submission regarding the need for protection of children (under 18 years) who were caught up in the criminal justice system. Other NGOs which made submissions including issues relating to children in trouble with the law were the Community Law Centre (UWC), National Institute for Public Interest Law and Research and Lawyers for Human Rights.

Court. The court found the juvenile sentence of whipping to be unconstitutional[8], and it was abolished.

In 1995 South Africa ratified the Convention on the Rights of the Child[9] without reservation. Articles 37 and 40 have been repeatedly referred to in discussions about a new juvenile justice system since that time.[10] (See United Nations International Convention on the Rights of the Child, page 146.) The point has been made that article 40(3) of the Convention obliges state parties to establish laws, procedures, authorities and institutions specifically applicable to children in conflict with the law. After ratification, the process of drafting an official National Plan of Action was commenced, and as part of this process a Justice sectoral working group was set up. The Justice sectoral working group recommended that the South African Law Commission should be requested to develop a juvenile justice system to give effect to the Convention.[11]

Other international instruments relevant to juvenile justice have also influenced debate and policy making[12] regarding juvenile justice in South Africa, notably the United Nations Guidelines for the Prevention of Juvenile Delinquency (the Riyadh Guidelines), the United Nations Standard Minimum Rules for Administration of Juvenile Justice (the Beijing Rules), and the United Nations Rules for the Protection of Juveniles Deprived of their Liberty (the JDLs).

The African Charter on the Rights and Welfare of the Child has also been referred to in the ongoing debates. Although the African Charter does not differ significantly in content from the UN Convention on issues relating to juvenile justice, it is sometimes favoured by South Africans because of its emphasis on

---

8   *S v Williams* 1995 (7) BCLR 861 (CC).
9   Adopted by the General Assembly on 20 November 1989, ratified by South Africa on 16 June 1995.
10 See generally Inter-Ministerial Committee on Young People at Risk *Interim Policy Recommendations* 1996.
11 South African Law Commission Issue Paper 9 *Juvenile Justice* 1997 1.
12 See generally National Institute for Public Interest Law and Research *Juvenile Justice Instruments* 1996; Inter-Ministerial Committee on Young People at Risk *In Whose Best Interests? Report on Places of Safety, Schools of Industry and Reform Schools* 1996; A Skelton 1996 *Acta Juridica* 180.

responsibilities corresponding with rights.¹³ The United Nations instruments promote a highly individualised approach to the rights of the child, whereas the African Charter takes a more collective approach, blending children's rights with respect for family and community. The approach of the African Charter accords well with the concept of restorative justice, and the trend towards restorative justice is a second sphere of influence which can be identified as having a major impact on the reform of juvenile justice in South Africa.

4 RESTORATIVE JUSTICE

Restorative justice is nothing new to South Africa. Although many may not be familiar with the term, the majority of South Africans will recognise the concept once it is explained to them. Restorative justice[14] is a theory of justice which relies on reconciliation rather than on punishment. It begins with the notion that a society which is functioning well operates within a balance of rights and responsibilities. When an incident occurs which upsets this balance, methods must be found to restore the balance, so that community members including the offender and the victim, can come to terms with the incident and can carry on with their lives.

In order for this to occur the offender must accept responsibility for the fact that his or her behaviour has caused harm to the victim, and the victim must be prepared to negotiate and accept restitution or compensation for the offender's wrongdoing. Thus the purpose of restorative justice is to identify responsibilities, to meet needs and to promote healing. South Africa's Truth and Reconciliation Commission may be described as an exercise in restorative justice on a massive scale. Long before the Truth and Reconciliation Commission, however, and long before apartheid and colonisation, restorative justice was known and understood by people living in South Africa. Rec-

---

13 See A Skelton (ed) *Children and the Law* 1998 30.
14 See generally H Zehr *Changing Lenses: A New Focus for Criminal Justice* 1990.

onciliation, restoration and harmony lie at the heart of African adjudication.[15] The central purpose of a customary law court was to acknowledge that a wrong had been done and to determine what amends should be made.[16] Community-based justice of this restorative nature was not peculiar to Africa, and a trend has been developing in a number of former colonies where indigenous people are living to return to restorative justice models.[17]

Interestingly, it is in the field of juvenile justice that many experiments with regard to restorative justice have been taking place. New Zealand has provided a striking example. During the 1980s the government of New Zealand decided that their juvenile justice system was due for reform. When a first draft of new legislation met with widespread criticism, especially from Maori and Pacific Island leadership, the government set up a working party to advise a parliamentary committee on how the bill needed to be changed. This working party travelled throughout New Zealand listening to the opinions of the public, including Maoris and Pacific Islanders.[18]

This process resulted in the Children, Young Persons and their Families Act, legislation which seeks to involve families and communities in making decisions about children who are accused of crimes and aims for negotiated solutions to conflict. The central mechanism is a 'family group conference' which is an alternative to taking children through the criminal justice system. The young person must acknowledge responsibility for his or her actions.

The procedure involves a youth justice co-ordinator, who convenes a meeting of all the people who are significant in the child's life, as well as the victim and persons supportive to him or her. The main goal of the conference is to formulate a plan for how best to put the wrong right. The eventual outcome is

---

15 A N Allot 'The people as law makers: Custom, practice and public opinion as sources of law in Africa and England' (1977) 1 *Journal of African Law* 21. See also T W Bennet *A Sourcebook on African Customary Law in Southern Africa* 1991.
16 C Dlamini 'The role of chiefs in the Administration of Justice' (unpublished LLM thesis, University of Pretoria, 1988).
17 A Skelton 'International trends in the re-emergence of traditional systems' in *Justice for Children: challenges for policy and practice in sub-Saharan Africa* 1998 99.
18 J Consedine *Restorative Justice: Healing the effects of crime* 1995 at 105.

agreed to by all the parties.[19]

The New Zealand system has been hailed internationally and many countries are experimenting with conferencing. Australia, Canada, USA and the United Kingdom are all piloting some form of community conferencing as diversion or sentencing options. Academics and practitioners in South Africa have, for a number of years, been following the development of restorative justice and of family group conferencing. In 1992 NICRO began to introduce the idea of diversion of children away from the criminal justice system, and promoted this concept by using the language of restorative justice.[20] In 1995 the Inter-Ministerial Committee on Young People at Risk[21] set up a pilot project on family group conferences in Pretoria. The project ran 42 family group conferences, testing the setting up of conferences, mediation, outcomes, community participation, and victim and offender satisfaction. The report[22] of the project provides a valuable resource which identifies the practical implications of making family group conferences part of a future juvenile justice system.

5 POLITICAL WILL

A third major influence on juvenile justice reform thus far has been the sudden injection of political will which the broader transformation of South Africa brought about. South Africa's first democratic elections in April 1994 led to the installation of the new government under the presidency of Nelson Mandela. In many early speeches he highlighted the rights of children, and in an address to parliament he said

---

19 A Morris 'Legislating for the effective involvement of young people, families, victims and the community in the juvenile justice system' conference paper delivered at the *International Conference on Drafting Juvenile Justice Legislation* hosted by the South African Law Commission at Gordon's Bay in November 1997.
20 L Muntingh and R Shapiro *Diversions: An Introduction to Diversion from the Criminal Justice System* 1994.
21 The Inter-Ministerial Committee on Young People at Risk was set up in 1995 to develop policy for the transformation of the child and youth care system.
22 Inter-Ministerial Committee on Young People at Risk 'Report of the Family Group Conference Pilot Project 1998.'

> 'The Government will, as a matter of urgency, attend to the tragic and complex question of children and juveniles in detention and prison. The basic principle from which we will proceed from now onwards is that we must rescue the children of the nation and ensure that the system of criminal justice must be the very last resort in the case of juvenile offenders.'

Juvenile justice reformists in South Africa quickly saw the opportunity of engaging some 'Madiba[23] Magic' to their cause. The words quoted above have often been used as a departure point by those working to develop a new juvenile justice system.[24] In addition, in the first few years after the elections a number of politicians and cabinet ministers have publicly shown support for the idea of a radical change in the criminal justice system as it relates to children.

The Minister of Justice, as part of his response to the Justice Sectoral Working group of the National Plan of Action for Children requested the South African Law Commission to include an investigation into juvenile justice in its programme. A project committee was set up and an Issue Paper was published in 1997 stating that legislation for a comprehensive juvenile justice system would be drafted. The Issue Paper is a showcase of the influence of children's rights within a framework of national and international human rights standards and of restorative justice. I quote a passage from the Issue Paper[25] which gives a broad overview of the vision:

> 'The South African Constitution and international instruments give an outline of what should be included in a future South African juvenile justice system. In line with these principles the project committee is of the view that the overall approach should aim to promote the well-being of the child, and to deal with each child in an indi-

---

23 Madiba is Nelson Mandela's clan name, and is used as a term of respect. See N Mandela *Long Walk to Freedom* 1994 at 4.
24 South African Law Commission *Juvenile Justice* Issue paper 9 (1997).
25 South African Law Commission *Juvenile Justice* Issue Paper 9 at 5.

vidualised way. A key aspect should be diversion of cases in defined circumstances away from the criminal justice system as early as possible ... The involvement of family and community is of vital importance, as is sensitivity to culture, tradition and the empowerment of victims. There should be an emphasis on young people being held accountable for their actions. This should be done in a manner which gives them an opportunity to turn away from criminal activity.'

The Issue Paper goes on to talk about children's participation in decision making, that when children have been tried and convicted by a court the presiding officer deciding upon a sentence should be guided by the principles of proportionality and the best interests of the child and that the deprivation of liberty should only be considered as a last resort. The description of the vision ends with the words, 'In line with national policy, the restorative justice approach forms part of the framework underpinning a new juvenile justice system'. The phrases which make up this description of the vision for a new juvenile justice system in South Africa are deeply imbued with an awareness of children's rights and blended with an understanding of restorative justice principles.

The fact that the South African Law Commission Issue Paper was warmly endorsed by the Minister of Justice when it was released in May 1997 showed that these ideas enjoyed political support at that time. At an international conference on drafting juvenile justice legislation in November 1997 political support still appeared to be intact. The Minister of Justice's speech prepared for the opening of the conference reflected a commitment to a balanced juvenile justice system respectful of children's rights. The Deputy Minister of Justice chaired the first session of the conference, and remained in attendance for much of the proceedings.

Now, however, in October 1998, the question of political will is not as clear as it was. The first signs that political will, although an important ingredient, is not in itself a foundation on which any lasting reform process can be built appeared in relation to the unfortunate history of attempts to bring about legal reform with regard to children awaiting trial in prison. At the end of 1994, only a few months into the democratically elected government's term of office, an amendment[26] was made to section 29 of the Correctional Services Act 8 of 1959. The amendment prevented the holding in police cells or prisons of children under 18 years for longer than 24 hours after arrest with the proviso that children over 14 and under 18 years charged with serious offences (which were listed in a Schedule to the Act) could be held for 48 hours. The aim of the legislation was that children should be sent home to await their trials. Where this was not possible the new law provided that they should be accommodated in a place of safety. Places of safety in South Africa are primarily designed and used for the temporary accommodation of children with regard to whom care proceedings are pending. They are therefore not 'lock ups' and the staff working in them are not trained to deal with children needing intensive management.

This first bold move of the South African Government to deal with the concern about children awaiting trial was not a great success. Little had been done to develop the infrastructure that was needed to make the law workable, such as extra or differentiated places to hold children who could not be placed at home, or the training and preparation of staff. As a result, there was pandemonium, with children absconding from places of safety all over the country, many failing to return to stand trial. All of this took place in a climate of increasing public concern about crime. There was a public outcry, enthusiastically broadcast by the media. The political will which had led to this first action on the part of the new government now began to waver. Only six months after the 1994 amendment had come into operation a private member's bill put forward by a member of the African National Congress proposed that, as a temporary and extraordinary measure, courts should be empow-

---

[26] Correctional Services Amendment Act 17 of 1994.

ered to order that certain children be held in prison to await trial. Thus a second amendment[27] was made to section 29 of the Correctional Services Act. This allowed for children charged with serious offences (listed in Schedule 2 to the Act) to be held in prison awaiting trial. In addition, the court could order the detention of any child over the age of 14 years in a prison, if he or she was charged with 'any other offence, in circumstances of such a serious nature as to warrant the detention'. The Amendment Act contained a savings clause intended to cause those sections allowing for detention of children beyond 48 hours to fall away after one year, or at the express wish of parliament for one further year. However, due to a drafting flaw in the savings clause those sections did not fall away in May 1998 as had been expected, thus the law as amended by the 1996 amendment remains in force.

The painful lesson which has been taught to juvenile justice reformists through this experience is that political will, although necessary, can never make up for thorough planning and provisioning. The loss of public support for children awaiting trial has had and will continue to have broad reverberations. Dirk van Zyl Smit, after describing this history of section 29 of the Correctional Services Act, concludes with the following observation:

> 'Although comprehensive juvenile justice with imaginative provision for community participation may still be introduced, the history thus far has made its acceptance less likely.'[28]

6 CHILDREN'S RIGHTS AND RESTORATIVE JUSTICE VERSUS CRIME CONTROL

This brings me to the pivotal question raised in this paper. Is it still possible to view juvenile justice through the windows of

---

27 Correctional Services Amendment Act 14 of 1996.
28 'Criminological Ideas and the South African Transition' 1999 *BJC* (forthcoming).

children's rights and restorative justice? Or are we moving towards a situation in South Africa where we will be forced to view it through the narrow keyhole of crime control?

Julia Sloth-Nielsen, in a conference paper[29] presented earlier this year, raised the question as to whether, in fact, the framework within which juvenile justice is being debated in South Africa has shifted away from a child rights issue to one of crime control. Crime and its control has become a pivotal theme in South Africa. South African policy and law makers have in recent years begun to embrace a number of ideas relating to crime control, primarily borrowed from the United States.[30]

The 'broken window approach to policing' championed by the former Commissioner for New York City, William Bratton, was discussed enthusiastically in the South African press. In the United States Bratton had achieved much success by exhorting police to 'crack down on the squeegee boys' – a reference to young (mainly black) males who washed car windscreens in New York streets.[31] This approach is somewhat at odds with the idea of diversion of children away from the criminal justice system.

Also from the United States of America comes the concept of mandatory minimum sentences – in the US federal code over 60 statutes contain mandatory minimum sentences.[32] At the end of 1997 the Justice Portfolio Committee voted in a Bill on minimum sentences. Although the minimum sentences in the South African Bill were not mandatory, in deference to our Constitution, the similarity of this Bill to the American approach of 'three

---

29 J Sloth-Nielsen, 'Past pandemonium, present peculiarities and future potential' presented at a conference 'Juvenile Justice: A counter-revolution' held at Quinnipiac College Centre for Child Law, USA, September 1998.
30 American crime control ideas have also been exported to England, where 'zero tolerance' and 'fast tracking' have become part of the language of dealing with youthful offenders. See further D Bedingfield 'Children and Crime' in *The child in need: children, the state and the law* 1998 at 479.
31 G Simpson 'Youth Crime in South Africa' a conference paper presented at a conference entitled 'Appropriate Justice for young people: exploring alternatives to retribution', hosted in Cape Town by the Institute of Criminology (UCT) and NICRO, 5 and 6 February 1997.
32 South African Law Commission *Mandatory Minimum Sentencing* Issue Paper 11 (1997).

strikes and you're out'[33] alerted criminal law reformists to the fact that we were moving away from a balanced human rights approach to an approach in which fighting crime was the overwhelming consideration. The South African Law Commission, earlier in 1997, had published an Issue Paper criticising mandatory minimum sentencing, and rejecting it as an option for South Africa. In a list of possible solutions[34] the Issue Paper includes presumptive sentencing guidelines, voluntary sentencing guidelines, principles of sentencing which determine the imposition of imprisonment, and as a final option 'the enactment of mandatory minimum sentences combined with a discretion to depart from the sentences under certain conditions'. It was this option, the most retributive of all the options offered, which provided the inspiration for what was to become the Criminal Procedure Amendment Act.[35] This amendment provides for minimum sentences ranging from a minimum of five years to life imprisonment for offences listed in Schedule 2 to the Criminal Procedure Act. Different sentences are prescribed for first, second, third and subsequent offenders. The sentences must be imposed unless there are substantial and compelling reasons (the onus of showing these rest on the accused). The presiding officer must give written reasons for deviating from the minimum sentence.

The initial draft of the legislation[36] included offenders under the age of 18 years within its ambit. Non-governmental organisations rallied and made both written and oral submissions on the draft bill to the Portfolio Committee on Justice, arguing[37] that the idea of minimum sentencing for children would go against the UN Convention and the South African Constitution which both state that the detention of children should be a measure of last resort, and that minimum sentences for children would in fact make imprisonment a first resort, notwith-

---

33 The US Federal Violent Crime Control and Law Enforcement Act of 1994 contains a three strikes provision.
34 South African Law Commission *Mandatory Minimum Sentencing* Issue Paper 11 at 52-54.
35 105 of 1997.
36 Bill B46-97.
37 A Skelton and J Sloth-Nielsen 'Submission to Portfolio Committee on Justice on Aspects of the Criminal Law Amendment Bill B46-97' (1997) unpublished paper.

standing the 'escape clause' which would allow the court, in its discretion, to deviate from the minimum sentence. Perhaps as a result of these submissions, the Bill was changed so that children under the age of 16 years are now completely excluded from the ambit of the Criminal Law Amendment Act, and 16 and 17 year olds, while included in its ambit, are treated differently in that the onus is on the state to show that there are substantial and compelling reasons why the minimum sentence **should** be imposed. The reason for this change seemed to be influenced by the argument that a minimum sentence of imprisonment linked to an onus on the accused would be in breach of the international and constitutional provision that imprisonment of children should always be a measure of last resort.

The efforts to exclude children from the effects of the new bail legislation did not yield the same positive result. In 1997 the law relating to bail was changed to make it more difficult for accused persons charged with certain serious violent crimes to be able to be released on bail. Submissions to the Justice Portfolio Committee requesting that the Bill should not include children within its ambit were not favourably considered. The final Act made no differentiation based on age – this legislation, like the legislation on minimum sentencing, is based on lists of offences, and underplays the individual circumstances of the offender.

A further example of how American crime control concepts are gaining ground in South Africa is the development of the Prevention of Organised Crime Bill.[38] In its definition section the Bill provides a number of factors to guide the courts in deciding whether or not a particular individual is a member of a criminal gang. One of these factors is whether the person 'resides in or frequents a particular criminal gang's area and adopts their style of dress, their use of hand signs, language or their tattoos, and associates with known criminal gang members'. This is a rather broad sweep, and may spell danger for many teenagers who, although not really involved in criminal gangs,

---

38 118-98. The Bill draws heavily on California legislation dealing with street gangs.

enjoy wearing clothing and bearing tattoos that make them look similar to the local gang. The definition also says that a criminal gang member may be identified by a 'parent or guardian' and this gives a clue to the fact that this legislation is aiming to draw persons below the age of 18 years into its web. Chapter 5 of the Bill creates a list of 'gang related activities' which in themselves constitute an offence for which a three-year prison term may be handed down by the courts. Membership of a gang may be regarded as an aggravating factor for the purposes of sentencing.

The most recent piece of legislation to be developed by the national legislature that has a direct bearing on the issue of juvenile justice is the latest Bill dealing with the detention of awaiting trial children. This Bill places beyond doubt the fact that the political will described earlier in this paper has been diluted by the political imperative to wage war on crime.

The strange history of the Bill is that it started out as an attempt to offer increased protection for children in the pretrial phase. In early 1998 it became apparent that there was a flaw in the saving clause of the Correctional Services Amendment Act,[39] and that section 29 of the Correctional Services Act dealing with the pre-trial detention of children would disappear when the Correctional Services Act of 1959 was replaced by the new Correctional Services Act. On 1 April 1998 a cabinet statement was released from the Office of the President which began with the words:

> 'The Cabinet has endorsed the position of government that children and youth awaiting trial should not be detained in prison or police cells. Cabinet has agreed to the following: That there will be a repeal of section 29 of the Correctional Services Act, that new temporary legislation with a more restrictive provision than section 29 on pre-trial detention of children will be established within the Criminal Procedure Act to replace section 29 of the Correctional Services Act.'

---

39 14 of 1996.

The first draft of the Bill[40] did two important things that were in line with the aim to further limit pre-trial detention. It removed the discretion of presiding officers to detain children on any offence in circumstances so serious as to warrant such detention. It also raised the minimum age below which children should be permitted to be detained in a prison from 14 years of age to 16 years of age.

When the Bill was considered by the Portfolio Committee on Justice substantial changes were made to it. The most dramatic effect was to remove entirely the minimum age below which a child may be detained in a prison. Previously, only children of 14 years or older were permitted to be held awaiting trial in a prison. In the current Bill, there is no minimum age below which children may be imprisoned – the age-based criterion has been jettisoned in favour of offence-based decision making. A last minute inclusion into the Bill by the Portfolio Committee on Justice was a clause providing that a child under the age of 14 years may only be detained in prison if the Director of Public Prosecutions or a prosecutor duly authorised issues a written confirmation that he or she intends charging the child with an offence referred to in Schedule 8 and that there is sufficient evidence to institute a prosecution. The Bill[41] then proceeded to the National Council of Provinces, where a further amendment was made by the Select Committee for Security and Justice, which added the following clause to a list of matters to be considered by the court before deciding on the pre-trial detention of a child: 'the age of a person, particularly if he or she is under the age of 14 years'. This amendment may have been made because of letters[42] sent to the chairperson of the Select Committee for Security and Justice which pointed out that children under the age of 14 years are presumed by South African Common Law to be *doli incapax*, and that they are deemed to lack criminal capacity until this presumption has

---

40 B at 59-98.
41 B at 132-98.
42 Letters were sent by the Child Rights Project of Lawyers for Human Rights, the Legal Recources Centre in Pretoria and the Human Rights Committee.

been rebutted beyond a reasonable doubt. The detention of such children prior to the presumption being rebutted might thus be an unlawful detention.

The crucial question of the minimum age of criminal capacity and the minimum age of imprisonment has still to be decided upon for the future juvenile justice system in South Africa. The Law Commission Issue Paper on Juvenile Justice tends to weight the debate against the retention of the *doli capax* and *doli incapax* presumptions, recording how the presumptions have failed to protect children in South Africa. A minimum cut off age below which a child may not be prosecuted, nor linked to actual criminal capacity is offered as a possible alternative. The advantage of this approach is the certainty which it brings. What the debates in parliament in the latter part of 1998 have highlighted is that decisions related to minimum ages need to be made with the utmost caution. An environment in which consideration of the age of the child is outweighed by consideration of the offence with which he or she is charged is a dangerous one for efforts to reform. A clear cut-off minimum age below which a child can be prosecuted might be set extremely low – or even removed – by the Portfolio Committee on Justice. This means that the examination of these issues must be made not only against the backdrop of commitment to children's rights, but also in the light of political realities.

7 CONCLUSION

In answer to the central question posed by this paper it must be conceded that it is no longer possible to view juvenile justice only through the windows of children's rights and restorative justice. However, to concede that juvenile justice is henceforth doomed to be viewed through the keyhole of crime control would be a derogation of responsibility. What is acknowlegded is that the perception of spiraling crime in South Africa, fuelled by the media, has created a climate in which juvenile justice reform is more difficult than it would have been two or three years ago.

It has been shown, however, that arguments based on children's rights have helped to hold out against the slide towards crime control.

Those committed to juvenile justice reform must rise to this challenge. We need to remain steadfastly committed to children's rights, and we need to continue to promote restorative justice principles. We need to use the international instruments and the Constitution. It may even be necessary to litigate. Academics should be writing about these issues, not in an abstract way, but in a manner that is firmly rooted in the political reality of our time and focused on providing arguments strong enough to stand up to the crime control onslaught. The rhetoric of children's rights is still on the lips of some politicians – and in the hearts of a few: we must hold them to the commitments they have made.

The political economy of child law reform: pie in the sky?

Julia Sloth-Nielsen*
Belinda van Heerden**

1　INTRODUCTION

The last two decades have seen a plethora of laws regulating different aspects of children's lives being introduced in South Africa. In fact, between the passing of the Child Care Act 74 of 1983 and the closure of parliament last year, no fewer than 20 pieces of legislation affecting children and families have been promulgated, regulating inter alia such matters as guardianship, domicile, family violence, adoption, the position of fathers of natural children vis- a-vis their offspring, education, juvenile whipping – and so the list continues.[1]

According to the recently released census statistics, 4,4 million children in South African (more than 10% of the population) are aged between nil and four years. Children aged between nil and 19 years form 44,22% of the overall population.[2] It is evident that the earnings of the approximately 9 million employed people in the country,[3] out of a population of over 40 million, together with other sources of tax revenue, have to

---
* Associate Professor, Community Law Centre, University of the Western Cape.
** Associate Professor of Private Law, University of Cape Town.
　 We would like to thank Debbie Budlender (Community Agency for Social Enquiry), Sandra Liebenberg (Community Law Centre), Annika Nilsson (Raddda Barnen (SA) and Shirley Robinson (IDASA Children's Budget Project) for their valuable comments on earlier drafts of this paper. The financial assistance of the Centre for Child Law (University of Pretoria) is also gratefully acknowledged by Belinda van Heerden.
1　See generally J Sloth-Nielsen & B van Heerden 'Putting Humpty Dumpty Back Together Again: Towards Restructuring Families' and Children's Lives in South Africa' (1998) 115 *SALJ* at 156.
2　Statistics South Africa *The People of South Africa Population Census, 1996* (Pretoria 1998).
3　Department of Finance *Medium Term Budget Policy Statement, 1998* (Pretoria 1998) at 45.

stretch to provide state resources on social spending in areas such as education, welfare needs and health care. The education budget is in fact the largest at R45,3 billion in 1998/9 (21,9% of the government budget), the bulk of this destined for children as the end users. The welfare budget for the same period is R18,9 billion (9,1%) and constitutes the fourth largest budget item of government expenditure.[4] However, over 90% of this will be paid out in direct transfers, in the main old-age pensions, leaving less than 10% available for spending on social services.[5] An amount of R2,7 billion has been projected as the amount that will eventually be expended on the new child support grant when it is fully implemented over the next five years. It is against this fiscal and demographic backdrop that the debate about resources for a new legislative framework for child care and protection is taking place.

2 BACKGROUND TO THE PROCESS OF CHILD LAW REFORM

As we have previously described elsewhere,[6] the process of amending the existing Child Care Act in the period 1994-1996 was characterised by controversy about the nature, scope and import of the intended amendments. The law reform process came amid two key developments: the adoption of first the interim and then the final Constitution, both containing unique clauses on children's rights; and second, the ratification of the United Nations Convention on the Rights of the Child in 1995, which provided an international legal framework for further domestic law reform. It became apparent, too, that the piecemeal approach to tinkering with the existing Child Care Act was unsatisfactory. Both international examples and the word-

---

4 Ibid at 71.
5 Department of Finance *Medium Term Expenditure Review (Welfare) 1998* (Pretoria 1998).
6 J Sloth-Nielsen & B van Heerden 'Proposed Amendments to the Child Care Act and Regulations in the Context of Constitutional and International Law Developments in South Africa' (1996) 12 *SAJHR* 247, 'The Child Care Amendment Act 1996: Does it Improve Children's Rights in South Africa?' (1996) 12 *SAJHR* 649.

ing of the Convention itself seemed to indicate that, at the very least, a complete overhaul of South Africa's legislation on child care and protection was called for, given the broad scope of obligations and rights provided for in the Convention.[7]

An important milestone was a conference co-hosted by the Children's Rights Project of the Community Law Centre and the Parliamentary Portfolio Committee on Welfare and Population Development in September 1996.[8] The conference harnessed the expertise of both lawyers and welfare experts from the government and the non-governmental sector, and also involved participants from African countries that are engaged in a similar process of law reform. Both the Deputy Minister of Justice and the Minister for Welfare and Population Development were keynote speakers at the event.

The debates were characterised by a focus on the position of children in difficult circumstances, the fragmentation caused at least in part by the lack of integration of legislation and common law, concerns about Africanising South African child law, and the need for an inclusive process of law reform with wide-scale consultation with stakeholders. Emphasis was placed on the necessity of adopting a realistic approach: crafting legislation which was affordable and indigenous (rather than borrowed from overseas); legislation which focussed on existing strengths inherent in our society; and probably most importantly, legislation with an odds-on chance of actually being implemented both by the executive and at grassroots level.[9]

The most significant proposal emanating from the conference was the suggestion that the South African Law Commission be requested to undertake the task of drafting recommendations for a review of the Child Care Act. And, in July 1997, at the express recommendation of the Minister for Welfare and Population Development, the Minister of Justice appointed a

---

7   South African Law Commission *First Issue Paper on the Review of the Child Care Act* Issue Paper 13 Project 110 (May 1998) chapter 1.
8   *Towards Redrafting the Child Care Act* Recommendations of a Conference of the Community Law Centre (University of the Western Cape) and the Portfolio Committee on Welfare and Population Development (September 1996).
9   Ibid at 33ff.

project committee from the commission for this purpose. Drawing together lawyers, including child rights experts and a children's court commissioner, child welfare experts, social work professionals and representatives from senior echelons within the Department of Welfare, as well as a senior researcher from the commission itself, this committee first set about examining the contours of its initial mandate to review 'the Child Care Act'. The consensus of the project committee members from the outset was that the task facing it was much broader and, in fact, that the first Issue Paper would raise the very question as to the appropriate scope of pending law reform in this area.

3 DETERMINING THE SCOPE OF A NEW CHILDREN'S STATUTE: RELEASE OF THE ISSUE PAPER AND THE CONSULTATIVE PROCESS

In May 1998, the Law Commission published an Issue Paper dealing explicitly with the scope of the proposed law reform endeavour. Asking for responses to exactly 100 questions, the Issue Paper addressed the challenge of how best to develop a systematic and coherent approach to child law consistent with South Africa's constitutional and international legal obligations of equity and non-discrimination and embodying the ideals of concern for the best interests of all children, participation of children in decisions affecting their interests and the protection of children in especially difficult circumstances.[10] For example, the Issue Paper, after providing a detailed problem statement and situation analysis of the position of children in South African society,[11] attempted to highlight the interface between the heavily interventionist structure underpinning the present Child Care Act and emerging policies of family preservation and autonomy.[12] Also, by emphasising the present fragmenta-

---
10 *First Issue Paper on the Review of the Child Care Act* chapter 2.
11 Ibid chapter 4.
12 Ibid chapter 7.

tion of statutory law and other provisions affecting children, the Issue Paper illustrated the fact that the intersection between common law and statutory law in this sphere can result in conflict and confusion, which can in turn negatively impact upon children's lives.[13] Further, in keeping with the inclusive and holistic approach that the committee wanted to promote, the Issue Paper also reviewed the position of children under customary law and under various religious laws.[14] The diversity of these laws and the imperative of ensuring that the fundamental principles underlying any new children's statute are, on the one hand, sensitive to customary and religious norms, yet on the other hand do not violate constitutional protections accorded all children, form the themes running through this part of the Issue Paper. Threads woven into the fabric of discussion about common and statutory law illustrate the changing definition of the family in modern law, the precise meaning of childhood and when it ends, and dilemmas associated with the fact that the law in South Africa (as elsewhere) has failed to keep abreast of technological change, particularly in the area of assisted reproduction.

In the final chapter entitled 'The Way Forward' the Issue Paper bravely engages with a discourse outside the traditional concern of legal drafters:

> 'Without detracting in any way from the potential significance and likely benefits to children of a new legislative framework in keeping with constitutional and human rights principles, the reservation has been expressed that (independent of the difficulties associated with the ensuring of the commitment of the resources required to underpin an effective child care and protection system), there are some aspects that legislation alone cannot achieve. For example, it cannot alone produce well trained, committed and motivated personnel who will bear the responsibility for the implementation of core provisions of the legislation, nor can it single-handedly change social, religious and cultural at-

---

13 Ibid chapter 6.
14 Ibid chapters 8 and 9.

titudes towards children. **Social and economic upliftment, too, are ultimately developments which occur outside the usual domain of legislative drafters, although much can be done in a legislative framework to ensure redress, equity and support for children in the most marginal situations.'**[15]

The crisp question is whether or not the committee's bold assertion with regard to the role of legislative reform in accomplishing redress, redistribution and support for children is in fact a valid one. Does this necessarily entail a massive injection of financial and human resources, which, as we argue later, is unlikely to materialise? Or are there other ways, within a legislative and policy framework, of capturing sufficient fiscal support to achieve the goals set for itself by the committee, and to fulfil community expectations?

The publication of the Issue Paper was followed by a consultative process without precedent in the law reform approach hitherto adopted by the South African Law Commission. Over and above the wide circulation of the Issue Paper, and the request for written submissions in response to the document, members of the project committee designed and hosted day-long workshops to elicit participation from ordinary people, ranging from school teachers, social workers and child care workers, to magistrates, the police, academics and representatives from non-governmental organisations. The workshops were presented in all nine provinces, in both large cities and more rural areas, and were characterised by the enormous interest they attracted. A dedicated worksheet, drawn up to facilitate the process of gathering informed responses to the topics raised for discussion, was utilised at the workshops. The information thus obtained was then analysed,[16] and will be incorporated in the next phase of the law reform process.

---

15 Ibid par 11.6 (emphasis added).
16 See *Report on Workshops held Nationwide to Discuss the First Issue Paper on the Review of the Child Care Act* South African Project Committee on the Review of the Child Care Act (1999).

What was particularly striking about the public reaction to the Issue Paper was the commonality of the themes that appeared to be of principal concern, despite the diversity of participants in the consultative process.

4 SIGNIFICANT TRENDS THAT HAVE SURFACED THUS FAR

4.1 Democratisation of the family and its internal relationships

Taking stock at the conclusion of this rather interim stage, it is possible to identify a number of significant trends that are likely to characterise the development of a new children's statute, whatever form such a statute eventually takes. We turn now to a discussion of these trends. Firstly, the notion of the shifting meaning of 'family' in South Africa,[17] which was raised directly as a point for discussion in the Issue Paper, struck a chord with a large number of respondents. For example, although there was heated debate for and against the possibility of recognising and providing for adoptions by gay and lesbian couples, there was a simultaneous acceptance (even among the dissenters) of the *de facto* reality of same-sex unions, and of the need to address the parenting position of partners in such unions.

Another interesting development relevant to the reconceptualisation of the family in South African law emerges from the introduction into our 'family law lexicon' of the concept of the 'primary caregiver', alongside the age-old terminology of 'mother', 'father', 'parent' and 'guardian'. The new notion emphasises the factual day-to-day care of the child, rather than any formal legal arrangement. In addition, it is delinked from the child's biological family, as also from any gender stereotypes. The recently adopted Welfare Laws Amendment Act 106 of 1997, which introduced the idea of a child support grant

---

17 And, as pointed out below, the fact that the construct of the family implicit in Western law has never reflected the reality of South African society.

being payable to the child's 'primary caregiver' in late 1997, seems to have been a catalyst in the rapid assimilation of the idea that the boundaries of the 'traditional' South African family are much wider than Western legal constructs have thus far permitted, and that new legal definitions are required to enable us to describe and regulate the status quo.

Within this broad framework of shifting **external** boundaries relevant to the conceptualisation of the family as a unit in society, there are parallel developments **within** the confines of the family structure.

As has become fashionable in many other countries of late, South Africa too has been forced to confront the potential abolition of the anachronistic hierarchy of power in the relationships between parent and child. At this stage, courts and writers in South Africa have already moved some way along the continuum, recognising that what was traditionally conceived of as 'parental power' over children is more properly concerned with the responsibilities of parents than with parental rights and powers.[18]

Children's autonomous rights have also emerged as a factor to be added to this equation. The question posed crisply in the Issue Paper is whether a new children's statute should leap the logical hurdle and attempt to provide a South African definition of parental responsibility, and, if so, how this would relate to the children's position within the family.

Given the fact that the UN Convention on the Rights of the Child, with its emphasis on the child as independent bearer of rights, appears to have entered the national consciousness, it is perhaps unsurprising that the feedback from the consultation process indicates an overwhelming consensus for jettisoning the authoritarian model underpinning the prevailing family law

---

18 See, for example, the dictum of Foxcroft J in *V v V* 1998 (4) SA 169 (C) at 176C-D: 'There is no doubt that over the last number of years the emphasis in thinking in regard to questions of relationships between parents and their children has shifted from a concept of parental power of the parents to one of parental responsibility and children's rights.' See also B van Heerden & B Clark 'Parenthood in South African Law – Equality and Independence? Recent Developments in the Law Relating to Guardianship' (1995) 112 *SALJ* 140 at 141-2.

dispensation.[19] This would undoubtedly have important ideological ramifications for our understanding of this sphere of the law, with ripple effects impacting upon divorce, parental control of children's lives and the position of fathers of extramarital children, to mention but a few examples. And, aside from the theoretical implications of such a shift, there may well be equally important resource implications: for instance, in the area of financial support for children by parents, increasing the focus on parental **responsibilities** has the spin-off (intended as a cost-saving exercise?) of also providing the philosophical justification for 'getting tough' with maintenance defaulters.[20] These and other resource ramifications, as mentioned earlier, will be explored further in the last section of this paper.

4.2 Ending the hegemony of the civil law?

An interesting dimension flowing from the possibilities inherent in the question of whether and how to legislate for the new 'democratic' family is the extent to which customary law and religious laws can be assimilated in this process. It is obviously desirable that a new children's statute should apply to **all** children within the country, independent of the system of personal law in which any individual child is raised. Of course, in seeking to achieve this goal, the law reformers are mindful of the fact that the integration of customary law with common and statutory law is an extremely difficult enterprise, and one which, to our knowledge, has not yet been achieved with any degree of real success elsewhere in Africa. Nevertheless, it seemed a goal worth pursuing.

However, interest groups that have been consulted on the questions raised in regard to the integration issue have been both vocal and consistent: there is clear opposition to perceived attempts to cross religious and customary borders, and to inter-

---

19 However, many workshop participants also bemoaned the decline in respect for family authority and the breakdown of systems of family discipline, perhaps an inevitable consequence of the political, social and economic upheavals so characteristic of recent South African history.
20 See *Report of the Lund Committee on Child and Family Support* (August 1996) chapter 5.

ference with deep-rooted cultural values, such as patriarchy – values that are sometimes difficult to reconcile with Western concepts of individual rights. As June Sinclair has pointed out, there is 'a substantial dissonance between South Africa's newfound extolling of individual rights and the promotion of a rights culture', on the one hand, and 'the [African] concept of human dignity, derived not necessarily through the relentless pursuit of individual liberty, but rather through membership of a group', on the other.[21]

While it remains possible that a future children's statute may contain a core of children's rights cutting across cultural and religious divides, such as a legislative entrenchment of the 'best interest' criterion, it appears likely that both customary and religious family law systems **as a whole** will prove resilient to external manipulation. It may well be that changes within these family law systems will ultimately come about more by way of response to political, social and economic developments on a macro level, than by any formal statutory intervention.

4.3 Invading the private law sanctuary

When one considers the nature of and responses to the debates raised in the Issue Paper, it becomes evident that the drafters of the new statute will have to contemplate, not just a comprehensive framework to regulate state intervention in child care and protection matters (i.e. the present ambit of the Child Care Act), but also how to determine the nucleus of family relationships in this country, and who gets to participate in such relationships. With this broad mandate, the new child law is likely to annex large chunks of the common law of 'parent and child'. Indeed, our traditional conception of the 'law of persons and the family' as falling primarily within the sphere of what is usually categorised as 'private law' is set to change radically.[22] The

---

21 See 'Ways of Seeing –"Lawyering" for a New Society in South Africa' in J Eekelaar & T Nhlapo (eds) *The Changing Family: Family Forms and Family Law* (1998) 493 at 505.
22 J Sloth-Nielsen & B van Heerden 'Signposts on the Road to Equality: Towards the New Millenium for Parents, Children and Families in South Africa' in Eekelaar & Nhlapo op cit 353 at 366.

new statute will marry diverse sections of legal concern relating to children and unite them in a predominantly public law environment. This idea has often been expressed in terms of the changing nature of the 'public/private divide' (although the continuing relevance of this dichotomy has itself been challenged). What remains to be seen is the extent to which the reshaping of private **law** as public **law** in turn has any bearing on the broader political, economic and social forces governing children and families. Will changes in the legal definition of a family result in changing the factual composition of families? Will entrenching gender neutral parental and familial roles in legislation promote greater social equality? More pertinently, will this law reform process make any difference to the channelling of state resources in the direction of the traditionally 'private sphere'?[23] The question of the redistributive potential of the law reform process is, of course, one to which we return in the last section of this paper.

4.4 Provisioning and governance

Another key theme raised during workshops was that of 'provisioning' for children. Time and time again, voices were heard to the effect that a Rolls Royce statute would make little real difference without the resources to underpin its implementation. But, at that same time, it is noteworthy that the potential and possibilities of the law reform process for better resourcing of structures and institutions for children was not lost on respondents. The thorny question of provisioning has recently

---

23 By way of illustration, are there lessons to be learnt from the recent reform of water law in South Africa? Until now, this area has been largely a matter of private regulation, with an emphasis on private land ownership, in accordance with principles derived from Roman law. The new National Water Act 36 of 1998 explicitly places access to water within the public law domain, and equally directly, links this to redistribution of a resource fundamental to economic and other development. Similarly the Employment Equity Act 55 of 1998 will intervene to enforce representativity (race, gender, disability and so forth) in the employment sphere. Previously a matter for the discretion of the individual employer, staff selection and promotion processes will henceforth become the subject of public scrutiny. As both of these statutes are very new, the effect of their implementation is as yet largely untested.

reared its head in relation to the amount the government was prepared to allocate to the child support grant. Only after forceful lobbying by a broad coalition of non-governmental organisations was the initial derisory amount of R75 per month per child below the age of seven years reluctantly increased to the current level of R100 per month per child. By the same token, it may seem obvious, but is probably still worth stating, that the determination of a host of important legislative issues in this child law reform process will be informed by resource considerations. So, for example, legislation mandating adequate access to education for children living on the street, the setting up of cluster homes for children infected and affected by HIV/Aids, the mooted increased role of the children's court as a central feature of child protective mechanisms, and effective support systems for children who are victims of abuse, is in reality underpinned by *a priori* budgetary considerations. In view of the above it should come as no surprise, therefore, that provisioning for a new children's statute has already taken centre stage in this legislative drafting process.

A related concern is one which we have termed 'governance'. This notion draws together a range of issues that are potential subjects for coverage in a future children's statute, such as whether or not we need to introduce stronger complaints mechanisms for children whose rights are violated (the idea of a children's ombudsperson comes to mind). And linked logically to providing channels for complaints from the ground, is the question of monitoring the application of all or aspects of the legislation, for example through provincial structures, a committee of the Human Rights Commission, or a statutory body along the lines of the Medical and Dental Council or the Independent Broadcasting Authority. The consultative process has brought out clearly from grassroots levels the clarion call for legislation that is backed by overarching control mechanisms, probably a reflection of the present degree of fragmentation experienced by workers in the field.

The conception of the notion of 'governance' does not end at complaints procedures and overall monitoring. Included in its ambit are decision-making and implementation structures at lower levels too. Thus, within the welfare sphere, the role of provincial departments in both resource allocation and service delivery appears to be a critical question to be resolved, as the repeated pensions crises (notably in the 'poorer' provinces) have amply demonstrated how differences in provincial approaches can actually subvert national strategies. Conversely, though, the emerging provincial protocols for the management and prevention of child abuse and neglect, which have been favourably received, tend rather to highlight the potential benefits to be derived from tailoring the legislative model to harness regional strengths and accommodate provincial diversity. We must also bear in mind that after April 1999, local government is set to assume a far more prominent role in governance than has been the case thus far.[24] Although the implications of increased responsibilities for this tier of government are still being explored, the prospect presents the drafters of a new children's statute with yet another variable to be considered in identifying the structures that will form the framework for implementation.

Integrally related to the executive competencies discussed above in relation to governance is the judicial arm of governance in the context of child legislation. Here numerous representations have been made and submissions received concerning the role of the judiciary in both a decision-making and supervisory capacity. Should the high court continue to be the so-called 'upper guardian' of children despite its inaccessibility to the vast majority of the South African population? Should the children's court continue to have the relatively limited functions of authorising the removal of children in need of care, and of determining placements of such children, without the concomitant powers of ongoing review of placements, and largely without either the power or the resources to introduce innovation and flexibility? And what of the possibility of mov-

---

24 This is due to the fact that the transitional arrangements concerning local government cease to apply on that date, and the powers of local government as contained in sections 151, 155, 156 and 157 of the final Constitution become fully operational (item 26(1) of Schedule 6 to the Constitution).

ing from a judicial model to a different model altogether: say administrative tribunals which include a range of professional voices, or lay panels, such as the widely acclaimed children's panels in Scotland?[25] Even more fundamentally, should a children's statute be weighted in favour of legal or quasi-legal solutions (orders, rulings, interdicts, and so on) to problems concerning parents, families and children, or are there more revolutionary possibilities that might be more appropriate in this part of the world? Something that springs to mind in this regard are current initiatives around family preservation pilot projects,[26] which clearly assume that any intervention is a matter of an ongoing process, rather than of any once-off, rule-based decision. In sum, the responses received indicate that no new children's statute is likely to be successful unless the challenges posed by 'governance' (in both the senses detailed above) are properly thought though from the outset.

5 REVENUE REALITIES

Throughout this paper we have alluded to the budgetary implications attached to the process of law writing upon which the committee has embarked. In an ideal world, law reform would be shaped by a concern for matters of principle, the bedrock of precedent, a desire for internal jurisprudential consistency, adherence to constitutional and international standards and an academic engagement with the niceties of one or other legal solution. Then, having exercised the necessary choices, the law reformers would be able to step aside, leaving matters of implementation and resourcing to the executive. But as the project committee has realised from the outset, this ivory tower approach to law reform is an indulgence that we cannot afford.

---

25 See, for example, A Cleland & E E Sutherland *Children's Rights in Scotland* 1996 at 96ff and L Edwards & A Griffiths *Family Law* 1997 chapter 8.
26 The Inter-Ministerial Committee on Young People at Risk *Report on the Pilot Projects* (Pretoria 1998) at 26ff.

5.1 A bigger pie?

Given that both human and financial resources are an essential precondition to the success of legislation, the reality is nevertheless that (irrespective of the form adopted of a new children's statute), the overall balance of state spending is **not** going to tilt more in favour of children, whatever the intentions of the government. The macroeconomic climate set by the government's Growth, Employment and Redistribution Strategy (GEAR) clearly abandons state economic intervention and public sector-driven redistribution as the primary mechanisms for the eradication of poverty. Rather, the emphasis falls on stimulation of private sector-led investment, to achieve an enhanced growth rate and improved job creation prospects. Along with this comes fiscal austerity (which suggests no immediate plans for bolstering the overall welfare budget in real terms). GEAR significantly prioritises economic growth and reduction of governmental expenditure and, in this context, there appears to be limited room to capture larger resources to benefit the poorest and most marginalised people in general and children in particular.[27]

This kind of thinking is not new. In 1996, one of the present authors reviewed the process of constitutionalising rights, and more pertinently, basic social and economic rights for children, and claimed that in the medium term, the overwhelming political support for the **idea** of children's rights would not necessary translate into measurable gains:

'... if a more widespread realisation were to develop that children's rights are not a "universal good" ... and that they indeed traverse significant political choices, commitment to potentially controversial long-term policies, and thorny questions about the allocation of scarce resources ... [c]hildren's rights issues may no longer be

---

[27] See *Public Expenditure on Basic Social Services in South Africa* Financial and Fiscal Commission Report for UNICEF and UNDP (Johannesburg 1998) at 21. GEAR targets are not, however, cast in stone, as the deliberations at the Presidential Job Summit held at the end of October 1998 illustrate (see for example *Welfare Update* (December 1998) at 3).

a wise or desirable political horse to back (although the "we support children" public rhetoric will no doubt continue). Given the uncontestable fact that children lack constituency and clout, and considering the mounting evidence of wavering political will, there are surely now substantial obstacles for further general achievements in the field of children's rights.' [28]

It is worthy of note that these predictions were made at a time before South Africa adopted what has been termed its self-imposed structural adjustment programme (GEAR), and indeed during the honeymoon period when there was still a general expectation that the new government would provide. Shortly after this, these fears were poignantly illustrated when the national NGO campaign to augment the proposed child support grant (by targeting more children, increasing the cut-off ages of beneficiaries, and raising the benefit level) met with limited success as the realisation dawned that more money was simply not going to be forthcoming.

5.2 Dividing the existing slices more effectively

A more pragmatic approach would be content with formulating a legislative model that would itself have an effect on resource distribution within the existing 'pie'. This is well illustrated by the example of subsidies to children in institutional care. As the Inter-Ministerial Committee on Young People at Risk reports,[29] the costs of maintaining a child in a residential care institution total R75 per day, with the direct subsidy per child amounting to approximately R800 per month. It could be argued that family preservation, rather than institutionalisation, is much more cost- efficient, enabling the same resources to reach a far greater proportion of children in a manner that is certainly

---

28 J Sloth-Nielsen 'The Contribution of Children's Rights to the Reconstruction of Society: Some Implications of the Constitutionalisation of Children's Rights in South Africa' (1996) 4 *International Journal of Children's Rights* 323 at 340.
29 In *Interim Policy Recommendations for the Transformation of the Child and Youth Care System* (November 1996) at 89-90.

more in keeping with the ideal of using removal and institutionalisation as a matter of last resort.³⁰

Also, the present amount per child transferred as a direct subsidy to children's homes and other residential care facilities is substantially more than the amount paid out in the form of an old-age pension to an indigent person (R500 per month from 1 October 1998). Indeed, it is eight times more than the amount payable to a caregiver caring for a child in his or her home, with the current level of the child support grant pegged at R100 per month. By weighting legislation **against** removal, monies might be freed up within the current expenditure framework to allow for greater emphasis in legislation and in practice for supporting children within their families and communities. However, care would have to be taken to ensure that the funds thus released are **in fact** utilised to provide the appropriate support for family care.

Another example flows from the present system of foster care grants. This grant, payable to a foster parent after a child has been placed in foster care by a children's court order, at present amounts to R360 per month. In 1996/7 alone the expenditure on these grants was R180 million.³¹ Yet no subsidy is payable for the more permanent placement option for children who cannot reside with their family in the long term, namely adoption. In addition, the pending Aids crisis has raised questions about the appropriateness of this kind of 'foster care' system (attracting a cash subsidy payable to an identified and designated 'foster parent'), where children in villages and town-

---

30 Of course, any such shift in resource allocation carries with it the real risk of increasing the cost burden to families and communities – often borne by women as caregivers. Non-governmental organisations have expressed the fear that the introduction of 'developmental social welfare' as a model for welfare service delivery and funding will have this effect. As one author points out: '[I]t is unacceptable and unsustainable for economic policy to be formed around an assumption that women's work will subsidise cuts in social spending.' (C Sweeting 'Women and the Family' (1996) 4 *Gender and Development* at 5-6, as cited by V Bozalek 'Gender Equality and Welfare Rights in South Africa: The Lund Committee on Child and Family Support' *Women & Human Rights Documentation Centre Newsletter* (April 1997) 3 at 4.

31 See J Kruger & S Motala 'Welfare' in S Robinson and L Biersteker *First Call – the South African Children's Budget* IDASA 1997 65 at 85.

ships whose lives will be most affected would benefit more from a broader form of support (with linked financial aid). The more fluid approaches that have been mooted are innovations such as neighbourhood centres offering a broad range of care services, or transfers of available monies to communities and villages as a whole, for the care of their young members as a **community** responsibility.[32] In other words, the question that arises is whether the present level of transfer payments for children can be more equitably shared to accommodate a greater range of child care arrangements.

But before tackling legislation that attempts to reorganise existing budgetary allocations, a note of caution must be sounded. Rumour has it that when the Lund Committee was briefed to investigate a more equitable and simplified grant system for poor children to replace the pre-existing state maintenance grant system, the sword of Damocles hanging over the committee was the very real risk that this type of grant could be abolished altogether. Aware of this, the committee consciously structured the proposals in such a way as to retain at least the same level of state spending in this area. The Lund Committee experience illustrates the possible danger of tampering too radically with inherited cost allocations, because proposals for change can be used by the government as an opportunity to jettison the old without implementing the new. It is a sobering thought that although the existing state maintenance grants have been cut by a third, and new grant applications are no longer being accepted, only 500 households are allegedly in receipt of the new child support grant: a very substantial saving to the state coffers, and no clarity about whether the savings thus effected can be rolled over to future years.[33]

---

32 See papers presented at the CINDI (Children in Distress) conference on ' Raising the Orphan Generation' Pietermaritzburg, June 1998.
33 See V Bozalek & A Parker 'The Impact of Economic Policies on South African Children' (unpublished paper October 1998) at 13. See further A Tilley 'The New Child Support Grant: Theory and Practice' (unpublished paper June 1998). The Department of Welfare is justifiably concerned about the low take-up rate for the child support grant (*Welfare Update* (October 1998) 1) and a tender has recently been advertised for the conduct of in-depth research into the phasing in of the child support grant (Tender number: Wel 36/98).

5.3. Partaking of someone else's slice

In the 1996 publication referred to previously, an attempt was made to identify certain 'support factors' that could assist in sustaining the momentum marking the implementation of children's rights in the initial stages of the reconstruction of South African society. Is it not possible to follow the same approach in the very process of conceptualising the economic frontiers of proposed child legislation in order to bolster the likelihood that such legislation has at least an outside chance of attracting the required fiscal support?

For example, one option open to law reformers might be to exercise choices so as to piggyback onto existing policies and programmes with already established public and state support, and therefore a virtually guaranteed source of funding. A case in point is the appropriate role of the children's court in a new statutory dispensation, an issue that has been canvassed above. This is not simply an academic debate to be viewed in isolation, given the present lack of capacity and low status of the children's court. To a certain extent the cards are already on the table. The establishment of family courts is more or less a *fait accompli*, and if the proposals of the recent Hoexter Commission,[34] as well as the stated intentions of the Department of Justice[35] are anything to go by, there is a very realistic prospect of expertise, services and material resources being channelled in the direction of the family courts. As the issues around the likely breadth of jurisdiction of the courts have still to be finally determined, it might be expedient to position a new children's forum within the family court structure, thereby tapping into an existing source of funding, rather than trying to dig a new well altogether.

Similarly, victim empowerment has been endorsed at the highest level of government policy. As a cardinal feature of the National Crime Prevention Strategy (which itself has a generous source of funding through the Reconstruction and Devel-

---

[34] Commission of Inquiry into the Rationalisation of the Provincial and Local Divisions of the Supreme Court *Third and Final Report* (December 1997) book 1 part 2.
[35] See, for example, Department of Justice Family Court Pilot Project *Concept Document* (November 1997).

opment Programme), it has been backed by a vociferous women's lobby. Not only has legislation dealing with family violence been promulgated,[36] and a project committee of the Law Commission been tasked with investigating victim empowerment more generally,[37] but at a purely practical level, plans are afoot to build and staff community support centres with the express idea of providing services to victims of crime. A new legislative framework around reporting and follow-up services in respect of child abuse could perhaps be formulated in such a way as to legitimately exploit this initiative.

5.4 Baking a new pie

Another strategy is to explore the avenue of new sources of funding. Although the room to manoeuvre at the national level seems limited, are there not possibilities of new resources to be accessed with the changes that are taking place in local government? Some metropolitan councils have already shown an awareness of their role in poverty alleviation and in redressing social inequality. For example, Cape Town has launched an initiative on street people (including children)[38] and a similar citywide endeavour has been started in greater Johannesburg. In Kwa-Zulu Natal local authorities are engaging in partnerships with *inter alia* the business community to address the plight of children with Aids.[39] Local government may not be directly involved in some of the types of resource allocation discussed above – grants, subsidies and direct transfers – but there are other possibilities, such as employment of community workers to serve children's needs, provision of capital resources for children's projects, and financial support to civic organisations that can in turn play an important role in implementing the new legislation.[40]

---

36 Domestic Violence Act 116 of 1998.
37 This falls within the ambit of the project on sentencing (Project 82).
38 Cape Metropolitan Council *Street People: Mission Statement and Recommendations for Local Authorities in the Cape Metropolitan Area* (June 1998).
39 See *Report of the Pietermaritzburg Summit on Children in Distress* (July 1996).
40 Care would have to be taken to ensure some level of equality across the country, given the disparities in revenue collection possibilities that characterise different local authorities.

Finally, as the experience of Uganda has shown, it is not impossible that the international community can successfully be mobilised to provide material support for the implementation of new children's legislation, particularly as the extensive children's rights framework enshrined in the Constitution is internationally regarded as something of a beacon to the rest of the developing world. Somewhat cynically, it could be argued that the international children's rights community has a 'moral stake' in assisting us to make these rights a reality.

6 CONCLUSION

In conclusion, the Law Commission Project Committee tasked with developing the new children's statute has been forced to confront the reality that this law reform process is not exclusively, or even primarily, a **legal** endeavour; on the contrary, it is a performance that must be played out on a much larger stage. It would appear that the 'words on paper' are in reality of far less import than the political and economic strategies adopted during the drafting process.[41] We anticipate that the kinds of tactics touched upon above will have an important bearing on the formulation of a new children's code: one which is politically acceptable, 'sellable' to the implementers of GEAR, and yet still achieves its primary purpose of protecting and empowering children in accordance with our obligations under the Constitution and the UN Convention on the Rights of the Child.

---

41 It is possibly a little unorthodox that this conclusion has been reached by two lawyers who were raised primarily on a diet of weighty legal tomes and voluminous law reports. However, in the interests of successful law reform, we have had to step outside our usual terrain, and engage (albeit as amateurs) with the mysteries of macroeconomic strategies.

United Nations International Convention on the Rights of the Child

PREAMBLE

The States Parties to the present Convention,

Considering that, in accordance with the principles proclaimed in the Charter of the United Nations, recognition of the inherent dignity and of the equal and inalienable rights of all members of the human family is the foundation of freedom, justice and peace in the world,

Bearing in mind that the peoples of the United Nations have, in the Charter, reaffirmed their faith in fundamental human rights and in the dignity and worth of the human person, and have determined to promote social progress and better standards of life in larger freedom,

Recognizing that the United Nations has, in the Universal Declaration of Human Rights and in the International Covenants on Human Rights, proclaimed and agreed that everyone is entitled to all the rights and freedoms set forth therein, without distinction of any kind, such as race, colour, sex, language, religion, political or other opinion, national or social origin, property, birth or other status,

Recalling that, in the Universal Declaration of Human Rights, the United Nations has proclaimed that childhood is entitled to special care and assistance,

Convinced that the family, as the fundamental group of society and the natural environment for the growth and well-being of all its mem-

SUMMARY: Preamble

The preamble recalls the basic principles of the United Nations and specific provisions of certain relevant human rights treaties and proclamations. It reaffirms the fact that children, because of their vulnerability, need special care and protection, and it places special emphasis on the primary caring and protective responsibility of the family. It also reaffirms the need for legal and other protection of the child before and after birth, the importance of respect for the cultural values of the child's community, and the vital role of international co-operation in securing children's rights.

bers and particularly children, should be afforded the necessary protection and assistance so that it can fully assume its responsibilities within the community,

Recognizing that the child, for the full and harmonious development of his or her personality, should grow up in a family environment, in an atmosphere of happiness, love and understanding,

Considering that the child should be fully prepared to live an individual life in society, and brought up in the spirit of the ideals proclaimed in the Charter of the United Nations, and in particular in the spirit of peace, dignity, tolerance, freedom, equality and solidarity,

Bearing in mind that the need to extend particular care to the child has been stated in the Geneva Declaration of the Rights of the Child of 1924 and in the Declaration of the Rights of the Child adopted by the United Nations on 20 November 1959 and recognized in the Universal Declaration of Human Rights, in the International Covenant on Civil and Political Rights (in particular in articles 23 and 24), in the International Covenant on Economic, Social and Cultural Rights (in particular in article ten) and in the statutes and relevant instruments of specialized agencies and international organizations concerned with the welfare of children,

Bearing in mind that, as indicated in the Declaration of the Rights of the Child, 'the child, by reason of his physical and mental immaturity, needs special safeguards and care, including appropriate legal protection, before as well as after birth,'

Recalling the provisions of the Declaration on Social and Legal Principles relating to the Protection and Welfare of Children, with Special Reference to Foster Placement and Adoption Nationally and Internationally; the United Nations Standard Minimum Rules for the Administration of Juvenile Justice ('The Beijing Rules'); and the Declaration on the Protection of Women and Children in Emergency and Armed Conflict,

Recognizing that, in all countries in the world, there are children living in exceptionally difficult conditions, and that such children need special consideration,

Taking due account of the importance of the traditions and cultural values of each people for the protection and harmonious development of the child,

Recognizing the importance of international co-operation for improving the living conditions of children in every country, in particular in the developing countries,

Have agreed as follows:

PART I: Substantive Provisions

Article 1

For the purposes of the present Convention, a child means every human being below the age of 18 years unless, under the law applicable to the child, majority is attained earlier.

Definition of a child:
A child is recognized as a person under 18, unless national laws recognize the age of majority earlier.

Article 2

1. States Parties shall respect and ensure the rights set forth in the present Convention to each child within their jurisdiction without discrimination of any kind, irrespective of the child's or his or her parent's or legal guardian's race, colour, sex, language, religion, political or other opinion, national, ethnic or social origin, property, disability, birth or other status.
2. States Parties shall take all appropriate measures to ensure that the child is protected against all forms of discrimination or punishment on the basis of the status, activities, expressed opinions, or beliefs of the child's parents, legal guardians, or family members.

Non-discrimination:
All rights apply to all children without exception. It is the State's obligation to protect children from any form of discrimination and to take positive action to promote their rights.

Article 3

1. In all actions concerning children, whether undertaken by public or private social welfare institutions, courts of law, administrative authorities or legislative bodies, the best inter-

Best interests of the child: All actions concerning the child shall take full account of his or her best interests. The State shall provide the child with adequate care when parents, or others charged with that responsibility, fail to do so.

Implementation of rights: The State must do all it can to implement the rights contained in the Convention.

Parental guidance and the child's evolving capacities: The State must respect the rights and responsibilities of parents and the extended family to provide guidance for the child which is appropriate to her or his evolving capacities.

Survival and development: Every child has the inherent right to life, and the State has an obligation to ensure the child's survival and development.

ests of the child shall be a primary consideration.
2. States Parties undertake to ensure the child such protection and care as is necessary for his or her well-being, taking into account the rights and duties of his or her parents, legal guardians, or other individuals legally responsible for him or her, and, to this end, shall take all appropriate legislative and administrative measures.
3. States Parties shall ensure that the institutions, services and facilities responsible for the care or protection of children shall conform with the standards established by competent authorities, particularly in the areas of safety, health, in the number and suitability of their staff, as well as competent supervision.

Article 4

States Parties shall undertake all appropriate legislative, administrative, and other measures for the implementation of the rights recognized in the present Convention. With regard to economic, social and cultural rights, States Parties shall undertake such measures to the maximum extent of their available resources and, where needed, within the framework of international co-operation.

Article 5

States Parties shall respect the responsibilities, rights and duties of parents or, where applicable, the members of the extended family or community as provided for by local custom, legal guardians or other persons legally responsible for the child, to provide, in a manner consistent with the evolving capacities of the child, appropriate direction and guidance in the exercise by the child of the rights recognized in the present Convention.

Article 6

1. States Parties recognize that every child has the inherent right to life.
2. States Parties shall ensure to the maximum extent possible the survival and development of the child.

Article 7

1. The child shall be registered immediately after birth and shall have the right from birth to a name, the right to acquire a nationality and, as far as possible, the right to know and be cared for by his or her parents.
2. States Parties shall ensure the implementation of these rights in accordance with their national law and their obligations under the relevant international instruments in this field, in particular where the child would otherwise be stateless.

Name and nationality: The child has the right to a name at birth. The child also has the right to acquire a nationality and, as far as possible, to know his or her parents and be cared for by them.

Article 8

1. States Parties undertake to respect the right of the child to preserve his or her identity, including nationality, name and family relations as recognized by law without unlawful interference.
2. Where a child is illegally deprived of some or all of the elements of his or her identity, States Parties shall provide appropriate assistance and protection, with a view to speedily re-establishing his or her identity.

Preservation of identity: The State has an obligation to protect, and if necessary, re-establish basic aspects of the child's identity. This includes name, nationality and family ties.

Article 9

1. States Parties shall ensure that a child shall not be separated from his or her parents against their will, except when competent authorities subject to judicial review determine, in accordance with applicable law and procedures, that such separation is necessary for the best interests of the child. Such determination may be necessary in a particular case such as one involving abuse or neglect of the child by the parents, or one where the parents are living separately and a decision must be made as to the child's place of residence.
2. In any proceedings pursuant to paragraph 1 of the present article, all interested parties shall be given an opportunity to participate in the proceedings and make their views known.
3. States Parties shall respect the right of the child who is separated from one or both parents to maintain personal relations and direct contact with both parents on a regular basis, except if it is contrary to the child's best interests.

Separation from parents: The child has a right to live with his or her parents unless this is deemed to be incompatible with the child's best interests. The child also has the right to maintain contact with both parents if separated from one or both.

4. Where such separation results from any action initiated by a State Party, such as the detention, imprisonment, exile, deportation or death (including death arising from any cause while the person is in the custody of the State) of one or both parents or of the child, that State Party shall, upon request, provide the parents, the child or, if appropriate, another member of the family with the essential information concerning the whereabouts of the absent member(s) of the family unless the provision of the information would be detrimental to the well-being of the child. States Parties shall further ensure that the submission of such a request shall of itself entail no adverse consequences for the person(s) concerned.

Article 10

> **Family reunification:** Children and their parents have the right to leave any country and to enter their own for purposes of reunion or the maintenance of the child-parent relationship.

1. In accordance with the obligation of States Parties under article 9, paragraph 1, applications by a child or his or her parents to enter or leave a State Party for the purpose of family reunification shall be dealt with by States Parties in a positive, humane and expeditious manner. States Parties shall further ensure that the submission of such a request shall entail no adverse consequences for the applicants and for the members of their family.
2. A child whose parents reside in different States shall have the right to maintain on a regular basis, save in exceptional circumstances personal relations and direct contacts with both parents. Towards that end and in accordance with the obligation of States Parties under article 9, paragraph 1, States Parties shall respect the right of the child and his or her parents to leave any country, including their own, and to enter their own country. The right to leave any country shall be subject only to such restrictions as are prescribed by law and which are necessary to protect the national security, public order (*ordre public*), public health or morals or the rights and freedoms of others and are consistent with the other rights recognized in the present Convention.

Article 11
1. States Parties shall take measures to combat the illicit transfer and non-return of children abroad.
2. To this end, States Parties shall promote the conclusion of bilateral or multilateral agreements or accession to existing agreements.

Illicit transfer and non-return: The State has an obligation to prevent and remedy the kidnapping or retention of children abroad by a parent or third party.

Article 12
1. States Parties shall assure to the child who is capable of forming his or her own views the right to express those views freely in all matters affecting the child, the views of the child being given due weight in accordance with the age and maturity of the child.
2. For this purpose, the child shall in particular be provided the opportunity to be heard in any judicial and administrative proceedings affecting the child, either directly, or through a representative or an appropriate body, in a manner consistent with the procedural rules of national law.

The child's opinion: The child has the right to express his or her opinion freely and to have that opinion taken into account in any matter or procedure affecting the child.

Article 13
1. The child shall have the right to freedom of expression; this right shall include freedom to seek, receive and impart information and ideas of all kinds, regardless of frontiers, either orally, in writing or in print, in the form of art, or through any other media of the child's choice.
2. The exercise of this right may be subject to certain restrictions, but these shall only be such as are provided by law and are necessary:
    (a) For respect of the rights or reputations of others; or
    (b) For the protection of national security or of public order (*ordre public*), or of public health or morals.

Freedom of expression: The child has the right to express his or her views, obtain information, make ideas or information known, regardless of frontiers.

Article 14
1. States Parties shall respect the right of the child to freedom of thought, conscience and religion.
2. States Parties shall respect the rights and duties of the parents and, when applicable, legal guardians, to provide direction to the child in the exercise of his or her right in a manner con-

Freedom of thought, conscience and religion: The State shall respect the child's right to freedom of thought, conscience and religion, subject to appropriate parental guidance.

sistent with the evolving capacities of the child.
3. Freedom to manifest one's religion or beliefs may be subject only to such limitations as are prescribed by law and are necessary to protect public safety, order, health or morals, or the fundamental rights and freedoms of others.

Article 15

Freedom of association: Children have a right to meet with others, and to join or form associations.

1. States Parties recognize the rights of the child to freedom of association and to freedom of peaceful assembly.
2. No restrictions may be placed on the exercise of these rights other than those imposed in conformity with the law and which are necessary in a democratic society in the interests of national security or public safety, public order (*ordre public*), the protection of public health or morals or the protection of the rights and freedoms of others.

Article 16

Protection of privacy: Children have the right to protection from interference with privacy, family, home and correspondence, and from libel or slander.

1. No child shall be subjected to arbitrary or unlawful interference with his or her privacy, family, home or correspondence, nor to unlawful attacks on his or her honour and reputation.
2. The child has the right to the protection of the law against such interference or attacks.

Article 17

Access to appropriate information: The State shall ensure the accessibility to children of information and material from a diversity of sources, and it shall encourage the mass media to disseminate information which is of social and cultural benefit to the child, and take steps to protect him or her from harmful materials.

States Parties recognize the important function performed by the mass media and shall ensure that the child has access to information and material from a diversity of national and international sources, especially those aimed at the promotion of his or her social, spiritual and moral well-being and physical and mental health. To this end, States Parties shall:

(a) Encourage the mass media to disseminate information and material of social and cultural benefit to the child and in accordance with the spirit of article 29;

(b) Encourage international co-operation in the production, exchange and dissemination of such information and

material from a diversity of cultural, national and international sources;
(c) Encourage the production and dissemination of children's books;
(d) Encourage the mass media to have particular regard to the linguistic needs of the child who belongs to a minority group or who is indigenous;
(e) Encourage the development of appropriate guidelines for the protection of the child from information and material injurious to his or her well-being, bearing in mind the provisions of articles 13 and 18.

Article 18

1. States Parties shall use their best efforts to ensure recognition of the principle that both parents have common responsibilities for the upbringing and development of the child. Parents or, as the case may be, legal guardians, have the primary responsibility for the upbringing and development of the child. The best interests of the child will be their basic concern.
2. For the purpose of guaranteeing and promoting the rights set forth in the present Convention, States Parties shall render appropriate assistance to parents and legal guardians in the performance of their child-rearing responsibilities and shall ensure the development of institutions, facilities and services for the care of children.
3. States Parties shall take all appropriate measures to ensure that children of working parents have the right to benefit from child-care services and facilities for which they are eligible.

Parental responsibilities:
Parents have joint primary responsibility for raising the child, and the State shall support them in this. The State shall provide appropriate assistance to parents in child-raising.

Article 19

1. States Parties shall take all appropriate legislative, administrative, social and educational measures to protect the child from all forms of physical or mental violence, injury or abuse, neglect or negligent treatment, maltreatment or exploitation, including sexual abuse, while in the care of parent(s), legal guardian(s) or any

Protection from abuse and neglect: The State shall protect the child from all forms of maltreatment by parents or others responsible for the care of the child and establish appropriate social programmes for the prevention of abuse and the treatment of victims.

Protection of a child without family: The State is obliged to provide special protection for a child deprived of the family environment and to ensure that appropriate alternative family care or institutional placement is available in such cases. Efforts to meet this obligation shall pay due regard to the child's cultural background.

Adoption: In countries where adoption is recognized and/or allowed, it shall only be carried out in the best interests of the child, and then only with the authorization of competent authorities, and safeguards for the child.

other person who has the care of the child.

2. Such protective measures should, as appropriate, include effective procedures for the establishment of social programmes to provide necessary support for the child and for those who have the care of the child, as well as for other forms of prevention and for identification, reporting, referral, investigation, treatment and follow-up of instances of child maltreatment described heretofore, and, as appropriate, for judicial involvement.

Article 20

1. A child temporarily or permanently deprived of his or her family environment, or in whose own best interests cannot be allowed to remain in that environment, shall be entitled to special protection and assistance provided by the State.
2. States Parties shall in accordance with their national laws ensure alternative care for such a child.
3. Such care could include, *inter alia*, foster placement, *Kafala* of Islamic law, adoption, or if necessary placement in suitable institutions for the care of children. When considering solutions, due regard shall be paid to the desirability of continuity in a child's upbringing and to the child's ethnic, religious, cultural and linguistic background.

Article 21

States Parties that recognize and/or permit the system of adoption shall ensure that the best interests of the child shall be the paramount consideration and they shall:
   (a) Ensure that the adoption of a child is authorized only by competent authorities who determine, in accordance with applicable law and procedures and on the basis of all pertinent and reliable information, that the adoption is permissible in view of the child's status concerning parents, relatives and legal guardians and that, if required, the persons concerned have given their informed consent to the adoption on the basis of such

counselling as may be necessary;
(b) Recognize that inter-country adoption may be considered as an alternative means of child's care, if the child cannot be placed in a foster or an adoptive family or cannot in any suitable manner be cared for in the child's country of origin;
(c) Ensure that the child concerned by intercountry adoption enjoys safeguards and standards equivalent to those existing in the case of national adoption;
(d) Take all appropriate measures to ensure that, in intercountry adoption, the placement does not result in improper financial gain for those involved in it;
(e) Promote, where appropriate, the objectives of the present article by concluding bilateral or multilateral arrangements or agreements, and endeavour, within this framework, to ensure that the placement of the child in another country is carried out by competent authorities or organs.

Article 22

1. States Parties shall take appropriate measures to ensure that a child who is seeking refugee status or who is considered a refugee in accordance with applicable international or domestic law and procedures shall, whether unaccompanied or accompanied by his or her parents or by any other person, receive appropriate protection and humanitarian assistance in the enjoyment of applicable rights set forth in the present Convention and in other international human rights or humanitarian instruments to which the said States are Parties.
2. For this purpose, States Parties shall provide, as they consider appropriate, co-operation in any efforts by the United Nations and other competent intergovernmental organizations or non-governmental organizations co-operating with the United Nations to protect and assist such a child and to trace the parents or other members of the family of any refugee

Refugee children: Special protection shall be granted to a refugee child or to a child seeking refugee status. It is the State's obligation to co-operate with competent organizations which provide such protection and assistance.

child in order to obtain information necessary for reunification with his or her family. In cases where no parents or other members of the family can be found, the child shall be accorded the same protection as any other child permanently or temporarily deprived of his or her family environment for any reason, as set forth in the present Convention.

Article 23

Disabled children: A disabled child has the right to special care, education and training to help him or her enjoy a full and decent life in dignity and achieve the greatest degree of self-reliance and social integration possible.

1. States Parties recognize that a mentally or physically disabled child should enjoy a full and decent life, in conditions which ensure dignity, promote self-reliance, and facilitate the child's active participation in the community.
2. States Parties recognize the right of the disabled child to special care and shall encourage and ensure the extension, subject to available resources, to the eligible child and those responsible for his or her care, of assistance for which application is made and which is appropriate to the child's condition and to the circumstances of the parents or others caring for the child.
3. Recognizing the special needs of a disabled child, assistance extended in accordance with paragraph 2 of the present article shall be provided free of charge, whenever possible, taking into account the financial resources of the parents or others caring for the child, and shall be designed to ensure that the disabled child has effective access to and receives education, training, health care services, rehabilitation services, preparation for employment and recreation opportunities in a manner conducive to the child's achieving the fullest possible social integration and individual development, including his or her cultural and spiritual development.
4. States Parties shall promote, in the spirit of international co-operation, the exchange of appropriate information in the field of preventive health care and of medical, psychological and functional treatment of disabled children, including dissemination of and access to information concerning methods of rehabilitation, education and vocational services, with

the aim of enabling States Parties to improve their capabilities and skills and to widen their experience in these areas. In this regard, particular account shall be taken of the needs of developing countries.

Article 24

1. States Parties recognize the right of the child to the enjoyment of the highest attainable standard of health and to facilities for the treatment of illness and rehabilitation of health. States Parties shall strive to ensure that no child is deprived of his or her right of access to such health care services.
2. States Parties shall pursue full implementation of this right and, in particular, shall take appropriate measures:
    (a) To diminish infant and child mortality;
    (b) To ensure the provision of necessary medical assistance and health care to all children with emphasis on the development of primary health care;
    (c) To combat disease and malnutrition including within the framework of primary health care, through, *inter alia*, the application of readily available technology and through the provision of adequate nutritious foods and clean drinking water, taking into consideration the dangers and risks of environmental pollution;
    (d) To ensure appropriate pre-natal and post-natal health care for mothers;
    (e) To ensure that all segments of society, in particular parents and children, are informed, have access to education and are supported in the use of basic knowledge of child health and nutrition, the advantages of breast-feeding, hygiene and environmental sanitation and the prevention of accidents;
    (f) To develop preventive health care, guidance for parents and family planning education and services.
3. States Parties shall take all effective and appropriate measures with a view to abolishing

Health and health services: The child has a right to the highest standard of health and medical care attainable. States shall place special emphasis on the provision of primary and preventive health care, public health education and the reduction of infant mortality. They shall encourage international co-operation in this regard and strive to see that no child is deprived of access to effective health services.

traditional practises prejudicial to the health of children.

4. States Parties undertake to promote and encourage international co-operation with a view to achieving progressively the full realization of the right recognized in the present article. In this regard, particular account shall be taken of the needs of developing countries.

Article 25

States Parties recognize the right of a child who has been placed by the competent authorities for the purposes of care, protection or treatment of his or her physical or mental health, to a periodic review of the treatment provided to the child and all other circumstances relevant to his or her placement.

Article 26

1. States Parties shall recognize for every child the right to benefit from social security, including social insurance, and shall take the necessary measures to achieve the full realization of this right in accordance with their national law.
2. The benefits should, where appropriate, be granted, taking into account the resources and the circumstances of the child and persons having responsibility for the maintenance of the child, as well as any other consideration relevant to an application for benefits made by or on behalf of the child.

Article 27

1. States Parties recognize the right of every child to a standard of living adequate for the child's physical, mental, spiritual, moral and social development.
2. The parent(s) or others responsible for the child have the primary responsibility to secure, within their abilities and financial capacities, the conditions of living necessary for the child's development.
3. States Parties, in accordance with national conditions and within their means, shall take appropriate measures to assist parents and others responsible for the child to implement this

---

Periodic review of placement: A child who is placed by the State for reasons of care, protection or treatment is entitled to have that placement evaluated regularly.

Social security: The child has the right to benefit from social security including social insurance.

Standard of living: Every child has the right to a standard of living adequate for his or her physical, mental, spiritual, moral and social development. Parents have the primary responsibility to ensure that the child has an adequate standard of living. The State's duty is to ensure that this responsibility can be fulfilled, and is. State responsibility can include material assistance to parents and their children.

right and shall in case of need provide material assistance and support programmes, particularly with regard to nutrition, clothing and housing.
4. States Parties shall take all appropriate measures to secure the recovery of maintenance for the child from the parents or other persons having financial responsibility for the child, both within the State Party and from abroad. In particular, where the person having financial responsibility for the child lives in a State different from that of the child, States Parties shall promote the accession to international agreements or the conclusion of such agreements, as well as the making of other appropriate arrangements.

Article 28

1. States Parties recognize the right of the child to education, and with a view to achieving this right progressively and on the basis of equal opportunity, they shall, in particular:
    (a) Make primary education compulsory and available free to all;
    (b) Encourage the development of different forms of secondary education, including general and vocational education, make them available and accessible to every child, and take appropriate measures such as the introduction of free education and offering financial assistance in case of need;
    (c) Make higher education accessible to all on the basis of capacity by every appropriate means;
    (d) Make educational and vocational information and guidance available and accessible to all children;
    (e) Take measures to encourage regular attendance at schools and the reduction of drop-out rates.
2. States Parties shall take all appropriate measures to ensure that school discipline is administered in a manner consistent with the child's human dignity and in conformity with the present Convention.

Education: The child has a right to education, and the State's duty is to ensure that primary education is free and compulsory, to encourage different forms of secondary education accessible to every child and to make higher education available to all on the basis of capacity. School discipline shall be consistent with the child's rights and dignity. The State shall engage in international co-operation to implement this right.

3. States Parties shall promote and encourage international co-operation in matters relating to education, in particular with a view to contributing to the elimination of ignorance and illiteracy throughout the world and facilitating access to scientific and technical knowledge and modern teaching methods. In this regard, particular account shall be taken of the needs of developing countries.

Article 29

Aims of education: Education shall aim at developing the child's personality, talents and mental and physical abilities to the fullest extent. Education shall prepare the child for an active adult life in a free society and foster respect for the child's parents, his or her own cultural identity, language and values, and for the cultural background and values of others.

1. States Parties agree that the education of the child shall be directed to:
    (a) The development of the child's personality, talents and mental and physical abilities to their fullest potential;
    (b) The development of respect for human rights and fundamental freedoms, and for the principles enshrined in the Charter of the United Nations;
    (c) The development of respect for the child's parents, his or her own cultural identity, language and values, for the national values of the country in which the child is living, the country from which he or she may originate, and for civilizations different from his or her own;
    (d) The preparation of the child for responsible life in a free society, in the spirit of understanding, peace, tolerance, equality of sexes, and friendship among all peoples, ethnic, national and religious groups and persons of indigenous origin;
    (e) The development of respect for the natural environment.
2. No part of the present article or article 28 shall be construed so as to interfere with the liberty of individuals and bodies to establish and direct educational institutions, subject always to the observance of the principles set forth in paragraph 1 of the present article and to the requirements that the education given in such institutions shall conform to such minimum standards as may be laid down by the State.

Article 30

In those States in which ethnic, religious or linguistic minorities or persons of indigenous origin exist, a child belonging to such a minority or who is indigenous shall not be denied the right, in community with other members of his or her group, to enjoy his or her own culture, to profess and practise his or her own religion, or to use his or her own language.

Children of minorities or indigenous populations: Children of minority communities and indigenous populations have the right to enjoy their own culture and to practise their own religion and language.

Article 31

1. States Parties recognize the right of the child to rest and leisure, to engage in play and recreational activities appropriate to the age of the child and to participate freely in cultural life and the arts.
2. States Parties shall respect and promote the right of the child to participate fully in cultural and artistic life and shall encourage the provision of appropriate and equal opportunities for cultural, artistic, recreational and leisure activity.

Leisure, recreation and cultural activities: The child has the right to leisure, play and participation in cultural and artistic activities.

Article 32

1. States Parties recognize the right of the child to be protected from economic exploitation and from performing any work that is likely to be hazardous or to interfere with the child's education, or to be harmful to the child's health or physical, mental, spiritual, moral or social development.
2. States Parties shall take legislative, administrative, social and educational measures to ensure the implementation of the present article. To this end, and having regard to the relevant provisions of other international instruments, States Parties shall in particular:
    (a) Provide for a minimum age or minimum ages for admissions to employment;
    (b) Provide for appropriate regulation of the hours and conditions of employment;
    (c) Provide for appropriate penalties or other sanctions to ensure the effective enforcement of the present article.

Child labour: The child has the right to be protected from work that threatens his or her health, education or development. The State shall set minimum ages for employment and regulate working conditions.

Sexual exploitation: The State shall protect children from sexual exploitation and abuse, including prostitution and involvement in pornography.

Sale, trafficking and abduction: It is the State's obligation to make every effort to prevent the sale, trafficking and abduction of children.

Drug abuse: Children have the right to protection from the use of narcotic and psychotropic drugs, and from being involved in their production or distribution.

Other forms of exploitation: The child has the right to protection from all forms of exploitation prejudicial to any aspects of the child's welfare not covered in articles 32, 33, 34 and 35.

Article 33

States Parties shall take all appropriate measures, including legislative, administrative, social and educational measures, to protect children from the illicit use of narcotic drugs and psychotropic substances as defined in the relevant international treaties, and to prevent the use of children in the illicit production and trafficking of such substances.

Article 34

States Parties undertake to protect the child from all forms of sexual exploitation and sexual abuse. For these purposes, States Parties shall in particular take all appropriate national, bilateral and multilateral measures to prevent:

(a) The inducement or coercion of a child to engage in any unlawful sexual activity;

(b) The exploitative use of children in prostitution or other unlawful sexual practises;

(c) The exploitative use of children in pornographic performances and materials.

Article 35

States Parties shall take all appropriate national, bilateral and multilateral measures to prevent the abduction of, the sale of or traffic in children for any purpose or in any form.

Article 36

States Parties shall protect the child against all other forms of exploitation prejudicial to any aspects of the child's welfare.

Article 37

States Parties shall ensure that:

(a) No child shall be subjected to torture or other cruel, inhuman or degrading treatment or punishment. Neither capital punishment nor life imprisonment without possibility of release shall be imposed for offences committed by persons below 18 years of age;

(b) No child shall be deprived of his or her liberty unlawfully or arbitrarily. The arrest, detention or imprisonment of a child shall be in conformity with the law and shall be used only as a measure of last resort and for the shortest appropriate period of time;

(c) Every child deprived of liberty shall be treated with humanity and respect for the inherent dignity of the human person, and in a manner which takes into account the needs of persons of his or her age. In particular every child deprived of liberty shall be separated from adults unless it is considered in the child's best interest not to do so and shall have the right to maintain contact with his or her family through correspondence and visits, save in exceptional circumstances;

(d) Every child deprived of his or her liberty shall have the right to prompt access to legal and other appropriate assistance, as well as the right to challenge the legality of the deprivation of his or her liberty before a court or other competent, independent and impartial authority, and to a prompt decision on any such action.

Torture and deprivation of liberty: No child shall be subjected to torture, cruel treatment or punishment, unlawful arrest or deprivation of liberty. Both capital punishment and life imprisonment without the possibility of release are prohibited for offences committed by persons below 18 years. Any child deprived of liberty shall be separated from adults unless it is considered in the child's best interests not to do so. A child who is detained shall have legal and other assistance as well as contact with the family.

Article 38

1. States Parties undertake to respect and to ensure respect for rules of international humanitarian law applicable to them in armed conflicts which are relevant to the child.
2. States Parties shall take all feasible measures to ensure that persons who have not attained the age of 15 years do not take a direct part in hostilities.
3. States Parties shall refrain from recruiting any person who has not attained the age of 15 years into their armed forces. In recruiting among those persons who have attained the age of 15 years but who have not attained the age of 18 years, States Parties shall endeavour to give priority to those who are oldest.
4. In accordance with their obligations under in-

Armed conflicts: States Parties shall take all feasible measures to ensure that children under 15 years of age have no direct part in hostilities. No child below 15 shall be recruited into the armed forces. States shall also ensure the protection and care of children who are affected by armed conflict as described in relevant international law.

ternational humanitarian law to protect the civilian population in armed conflicts, States Parties shall take all feasible measures to ensure protection and care of children who are affected by an armed conflict.

Article 39

Rehabilitative care: The State has an obligation to ensure that child victims of armed conflicts, torture, neglect, maltreatment or exploitation receive appropriate treatment for their recovery and social reintegration.

States Parties shall take all appropriate measures to promote physical and psychological recovery and social reintegration of a child victim of: any form of neglect, exploitation, or abuse; torture or any other form of cruel, inhuman or degrading treatment or punishment; or armed conflicts. Such recovery and reintegration shall take place in an environment which fosters the health, self-respect and dignity of the child.

Article 40

Administration of juvenile justice: A child in conflict with the law has the right to treatment which promotes the child's sense of dignity and worth, takes the child's age into account and aims at his or her reintegration into society. The child is entitled to basic guarantees as well as legal or other assistance for his or her defence. Judicial proceedings and institutional placements shall be avoided wherever possible.

1. States Parties recognize the right of every child alleged as, accused of, or recognized as having infringed the penal law to be treated in a manner consistent with the promotion of the child's sense of dignity and worth, which reinforces the child's respect for the human rights and fundamental freedoms of others and which takes into account the child's age and the desirability of promoting the child's reintegration and the child's assuming a constructive role in society.
2. To this end, and having regard to the relevant provisions of international instruments, States Parties shall, in particular, ensure that:
    (a) No child shall be alleged as, be accused of, or recognized as having infringed the penal law by reason of acts or omissions that were not prohibited by national or international law at the time they were committed;
    (b) Every child alleged as or accused of having infringed the penal law has at least the following guarantees:
      (i) To be presumed innocent until proven guilty according to law;
      (ii) To be informed promptly and directly of the charges against him or her, and, if appropriate, through

his or her parents or legal guardians, and to have legal or other appropriate assistance in the preparation and presentation of his or her defence;
(iii) To have the matter determined without delay by a competent, independent and impartial authority or judicial body in a fair hearing according to law, in the presence of legal or other appropriate assistance and, unless it is considered not to be in the best interest of the child, in particular, taking into account his or her age or situation, his or her parents or legal guardians;
(iv) Not to be compelled to give testimony or to confess guilt; to examine or have examined adverse witnesses and to obtain the participation and examination of witnesses on his or her behalf under conditions of equality;
(v) If considered to have infringed the penal law, to have this decision and any measures imposed in consequence thereof reviewed by a higher competent, independent and impartial authority or judicial body according to law;
(vi) To have the free assistance of an interpreter if the child cannot understand or speak the language used;
(vii) To have his or her privacy fully respected at all stages of the proceedings.
3. States Parties shall seek to promote the establishment of laws, procedures, authorities and institutions specifically applicable to children alleged as, accused of, or recognized as having infringed the penal law, and, in particular:
   (a) the establishment of a minimum age below which children shall be presumed not to have the capacity to infringe the penal law;

(b) whenever appropriate and desirable, measures for dealing with such children without resorting to judicial proceedings, providing that human rights and legal safeguards are fully respected.

4. A variety of dispositions, such as care, guidance and supervision orders; counselling; probation; foster care; education and vocational training programmes and other alternatives to institutional care shall be available to ensure that children are dealt with in a manner appropriate to their well-being and proportionate both to their circumstances and the offence.

Article 41

> **Respect for higher standards:** Wherever standards set in applicable national and international law relevant to the rights of the child that are higher than those in this Convention, the higher standard shall always apply.

Nothing in the present Convention shall affect any provisions which are more conducive to the realization of the rights of the child and which may be contained in:
(a) The law of a State Party; or
(b) International law in force for that State.

PART II: Implementation and Monitoring

> **The provisions of articles 42-54 notably foresee:**
> (i) the State's obligation to make the rights contained in this Convention widely known to both adults and children.
> (ii) the setting up of a Committee on the Rights of the Child composed of 10 experts, which will consider reports that States Parties to the Convention are to submit two years after ratification and every five years thereafter. The Convention enters into force – and the Committee would

Article 42

States Parties undertake to make the principles and provisions of the Convention widely known, by appropriate and active means, to adults and children alike.

Article 43

1. For the purpose of examining the progress made by States Parties in achieving the realization of the obligations undertaken in the present Convention, there shall be established a Committee on the Rights of the Child, which shall carry out the functions hereinafter provided.

2. The Committee shall consist of 10 experts of high moral standing and recognized competence in the field covered by this Convention. The members of the Committee shall be elected by States Parties from among their nationals and shall serve in their personal capacity, consideration being given to equitable geographical distribution, as well as to the principal legal systems.
3. The members of the Committee shall be elected by secret ballot from a list of persons nominated by States Parties. Each State Party may nominate one person from among its own nationals.
4. The initial election to the Committee shall be held no later than six months after the date of the entry into force of the present Convention and thereafter every second year. At least four months before the date of each election, the Secretary-General of the United Nations shall address a letter to States Parties inviting them to submit their nominations within two months. The Secretary-General shall subsequently prepare a list in alphabetical order of all persons thus nominated, indicating States Parties which have nominated them, and shall submit it to the States Parties to the present Convention.
5. The elections shall be held at meetings of States Parties convened by the Secretary-General at United Nations Headquarters. At those meetings, for which two thirds of States Parties shall constitute a quorum, the persons elected to the Committee shall be those who obtain the largest number of votes and an absolute majority of the votes of the representatives of States Parties present and voting.
6. The members of the Committee shall be elected for a term of four years. They shall be eligible for re-election if renominated. The term of five of the members elected at the first election shall expire at the end of two years; immediately after the first election, the names of these five members shall be chosen by lot by the Chairman of the meeting.
7. If a member of the Committee dies or resigns or declares that for any other cause he or she

therefore be set up – once 20 countries have ratified it.
(iii) States Parties are to make their reports widely available.
(iv) The Committee may propose that special studies be undertaken on specific issues relating to the rights of the child, and may make its evaluations known to each State Party concerned as well as to the UN General Assembly.
(v) In order to "foster the effective implementation of the Convention and to encourage international co-operation," the specialized agencies of the UN – such as the International Labour Organisation (ILO), World Health Organization (WHO) and United Nations Educational, Scientific and Cultural Organization (UNESCO) – and UNICEF would be able to attend the meetings of the Committee. Together with any other body recognized as 'competent', including non-governmental organizations (NGOs) in consultative status with the UN and UN organs such as the United Nations High Commissioner for Refugees (UNHCR), they can submit pertinent information to the Committee and be asked to advise on the optimal implementation of the Convention.

can no longer perform the duties of the Committee, the State Party which nominated the member shall appoint another expert from among its nationals to serve for the remainder of the term, subject to the approval of the Committee.
8. The Committee shall establish its own rules of procedure.
9. The Committee shall elect its officers for a period of two years.
10. The meetings of the Committee shall normally be held at United Nations Headquarters or at any other convenient place as determined by the Committee. The Committee shall normally meet annually. The duration of the meetings of the Committee shall be determined, and reviewed, if necessary, by a meeting of the States Parties to the present Convention, subject to the approval of the General Assembly.
11. The Secretary-General of the United Nations shall provide the necessary staff and facilities for the effective performance of the functions of the Committee under the present Convention.
12. With the approval of the General Assembly, the members of the Committee established under the present Convention shall receive emoluments from the United Nations resources on such terms and conditions as the Assembly may decide.

Article 44
1. States Parties undertake to submit to the Committee, through the Secretary-General of the United Nations, reports on the measures they have adopted which give effect to the rights recognized herein and on the progress made on the enjoyment of those rights:
    (a) Within two years of the entry into force of the Convention for the State Party concerned,
    (b) Thereafter every five years.
2. Reports made under the present article shall indicate factors and difficulties, if any, affecting the degree of fulfilment of the obligations under the present Convention. Reports shall also contain sufficient information to provide

the Committee with a comprehensive understanding of the implementation of the Convention in the country concerned.
3. A State Party which has submitted a comprehensive initial report to the Committee need not in its subsequent reports submitted in accordance with paragraph 1(b) of the present article repeat basic information previously provided.
4. The Committee may request from States Parties further information relevant to the implementation of the Convention.
5. The Committee shall submit to the General Assembly, through the Economic and Social Council, every two years, reports on its activities.
6. States Parties shall make their reports widely available to the public in their own countries.

Article 45

In order to foster the effective implementation of the Convention and to encourage international co-operation in the field covered by the Convention:
(a) The specialized agencies, the United Nations Children's Fund and other United Nations organs shall be entitled to be represented at the consideration of the implementation of such provisions of the present Convention as fall within the scope of their mandate. The Committee may invite the specialized agencies, the United Nations Children's Fund and other competent bodies as it may consider appropriate to provide expert advice on the implementation of the Convention in areas falling within the scope of their respective mandates. The Committee may invite the specialized agencies, the United Nations Children's Fund and other United Nations organs to submit reports on the implementation of the Convention in areas falling within the scope of their activities;
(b) The Committee shall transmit, as it may consider appropriate, to the specialized

agencies, the United Nations Children's Fund and other competent bodies, any reports from States Parties that contain a request, or indicate a need, for technical advice or assistance, along with the Committee's observations and suggestions, if any, on these requests or indications;

(c) The Committee may recommend to the General Assembly to request the Secretary-General to undertake on its behalf studies on specific issues relating to the rights of the child;

(d) The Committee may make suggestions and general recommendations based on information received pursuant to articles 44 and 45 of the present Convention. Such suggestions and general recommendations shall be transmitted to any State Party concerned and reported to the General Assembly, together with comments, if any, from States Parties.

PART III: Final Clauses

Article 46

The present Convention shall be open for signature by all States.

Article 47

The present Convention is subject to ratification. Instruments of ratification shall be deposited with the Secretary-General of the United Nations.

Article 48

The present Convention shall remain open for accession by any State. The instruments of accession shall be deposited with the Secretary-General of the United Nations.

Article 49

1. The present Convention shall enter into force

on the thirtieth day following the date of deposit with the Secretary-General of the United Nations of the twentieth instrument of ratification or accession.
2. For each State ratifying or acceding to the Convention after the deposit of the twentieth instrument of ratification or accession, the Convention shall enter into force on the thirtieth day after the deposit by such State of its instrument of ratification or accession.

Article 50
1. Any State Party may propose an amendment and file it with the Secretary-General of the United Nations. The Secretary-General shall thereupon communicate the proposed amendment to States Parties, with a request that they indicate whether they favour a conference of States Parties for the purpose of considering and voting upon the proposals. In the event that, within four months from the date of such communication, at least one third of the States Parties favour such a conference, the Secretary-General shall convene the conference under the auspices of the United Nations. Any amendment adopted by a majority of States Parties present and voting at the conference shall be submitted to the General Assembly for approval.
2. An amendment adopted in accordance with paragraph 1 of the present article shall enter into force when it has been approved by the General Assembly of the United Nations and accepted by a two-thirds majority of States Parties.
3. When an amendment enters into force, it shall be binding on those States Parties which have accepted it, other States Parties still being bound by the provisions of the present Convention and any earlier amendments which they have accepted.

Article 51
1. The Secretary-General of the United Nations shall receive and circulate to all States the text of reservations made by States at the time of ratification or accession.

2. A reservation incompatible with the object and purpose of the present Convention shall not be permitted.
3. Reservations may be withdrawn at any time by notification to that effect addressed to the Secretary-General of the United Nations, who shall then inform all States. Such notification shall take effect on the date on which it is received by the Secretary-General.

Article 52

A State Party may denounce the present Convention by written notification to the Secretary-General of the United Nations. Denunciation becomes effective one year after the date of receipt of the notification by the Secretary-General.

Article 53

The Secretary-General of the United Nations is designated as the depositary of the present Convention.

Article 54

The original of the present Convention, of which the Arabic, Chinese, English, French, Russian and Spanish texts are equally authentic, shall be deposited with the Secretary-General of the United Nations.

In witness thereof the undersigned plenipotentiaries, being duly authorized thereto by their respective Governments, have signed the present Convention.